BETTY CROCKER'S
meatless main dishes

GOLDEN PRESS / NEW YORK
Western Publishing Company, Inc.
Racine, Wisconsin

Front Cover
Top row: Chicken à la King, Home-Style Scrambled Eggs, Easy Chicken Gumbo.
Bottom row: Creole Flounder, Chicken Provincial, Tuna Dinner in a Dish.
Back Cover
Top row: Chicken Tetrazzini, Cheese Soufflé Deluxe, Salmon Romanoff.
Bottom row: Tuna with Noodles, Three-Bean Cassoulet, Garden Supper Casserole.

First Printing, 1973

Copyright © 1973 by General Mills, Inc., Minneapolis, Minnesota. All rights reserved. No portion of this book may be reprinted or reproduced in any form or any manner without the written permission of the publishers, except by a reviewer who wishes to quote brief passages in connection with a review. Printed in the U.S.A. by Western Publishing Company, Inc. Published by Golden Press, New York, New York.

Library of Congress Catalog Card Number: 73-86124

contents

going meatless

No money for meat? Then it's time to be practical and change your point of view. Switch your emphasis to the meatless sources of protein that won't break the budget, and schedule those costlier red meats—like beef, pork and lamb—in between. It's a happy compromise, really, because mealtime can be beautiful with Meatless Main Dishes. And this practical little cookbook will prove it to you.

Consider, for example, the many protein substitutes for red meat. There are Sunday's chicken and the Thanksgiving turkey, welcome anytime and for any occasion. Fish and seafood, so popular today that restaurants are built in their honor. Cheese and eggs that go to any meal of the day. And the humble dried bean, never to be outdone as a budget stretcher. These are the superstars of the meatless world. And all of them are so thrifty and versatile that we have based this whole cookbook on them.

But why call them superstars? Because of their high-quality protein. The fact is that lower-priced poultry, fish, eggs and cheese are equally good as protein sources as red meat. Also, dried beans are recognized as occasional alternates for red meat. Very good credentials, don't you think? And there's no shortage on variety.

So the question remains—how far do you have to go in the compromise? Meatless every day, every other day or just one day a week? Only you know that answer, but this we can assure you. Learn to make the most of the meatless foods and there will be no strain on anybody's appetite, no drain on the budget.

The name of the game? Same as the name of this cookbook, Meatless Main Dishes. And our budget-beating combinations? Casseroles, skillet dishes, soups and salads, for the most part, which place their emphasis on poultry, fish, cheese, eggs and beans. But to give you the greatest mileage from these high-protein foods, many of our main dishes also include extender foods like vegetables, rice and pasta. These Meatless Main Dishes are your main courses or the centers of attraction for your budget meals. According to your personal tastes, you plan your menus around them.

The cost factor Main dishes, even when meatless, usually take the larger share of the food dollar. Some are more costly than others, of course. Poultry goes strictly thrifty in our recipe for Chicken Pot Pie, page 18. But poultry combines with numerous ingredients and costs go up in the recipe for Turkey Mock Stroganoff, page 26. Prices will vary with fish dishes, too. Tuna Dinner in a Dish, page 31, comes in at a real bargain. But Shrimp and Mushrooms, page 46? When it's a long, long way till payday, save it till then and celebrate. And to cut corners with all these recipes, consider the following as essential.

Plan ahead Check the food pages of your newspaper before you shop—even lower-priced meatless foods cost more one day than another. Plot your menus to focus on seasonal buys—most fresh fish and shellfish, for instance, cost less during certain seasons. Carry a shopping list to curb any impulse buying. And learn to recognize the bargains.

Scout for bargains When you shop for the best buy on poultry, remember this: Large meaty birds are usually better buys than small ones. Also, chicken sold whole often costs less per pound than chicken cut up. It figures, doesn't it? You do the cutting.

Does this surprise you about fish? Frozen fish and shellfish are sometimes less expensive than fresh. Larger sized cans of fish offer considerable savings. Also, the kind of meat and style of pack affect prices on canned tuna (see page 34).

Be wise about cheese costs, too. Process cheese is a better buy in food value than process cheese spread at the same price; there's less moisture in the former. Mild natural cheese costs less than aged or sharp natural, process cheese less than mild natural, and almost any domestic cheese less than imported kinds. Size and packaging also count; wedges and sticks are less expensive than slices or shredded cheese. And you can save extra pennies on fancy cream or cottage cheese by adding your own chives, pineapple or onion.

Even eggs have their price advantages. In general, large eggs are a better buy than small ones, especially when there's less than 7¢ difference in consecutive grading sizes. And remember, the color of the shell has nothing to do with food value or cost.

Short course on protein There are two kinds of protein foods to think about. Foods of animal origin—which include meat, poultry, fish, cheese, eggs and milk—are higher-quality or complete protein foods. But foods of vegetable origin—nuts, grains, vegetables and fruits—are lower-quality or incomplete protein foods. Both kinds are needed every day, and there is a smart way to make them work together.

The trick is to team up an incomplete protein food—macaroni, for example—with one of the complete protein foods, like cheese. Then the protein value of the macaroni becomes more effective (recipe on page 58). The same goes for vegetables in partnership with chicken in Chicken Chow Mein, page 12. Or rice with tuna in our recipe for One-Dish Tuna and Rice, page 29. A shrewd strategy, you will note, for stretching food dollars!

The protein count Each of our Meatless Main Dishes is designed to provide one-fourth or more of an adult's daily protein needs, or at least 16 grams protein per serving.* At the end of each recipe in this cookbook, you'll find the grams protein per serving. It is a special feature with this book, and we hope you find it a helpful gauge for plotting the day's protein needs.

Naturally, you need more than one main dish to get your daily quota of protein, so you'll fill in with other main dishes and

*This amount is based on the Recommended Dietary Allowances (RDA) of 65 grams a day.

good accessory foods. Unless you prefer adding up the protein grams, we suggest the best way to complete a day's protein needs is by choosing a widely varied diet.

Push the penny pinchers Eyes right, please, and meet the protein punchers. Six groups of popular meatless foods that usually offer the best bargains for rounding out the day's protein needs. Prices vary, of course, and you may spot better buys. So take these as clues and add ideas of your own.

Starting with milk and friends, your instant cooking companions. Drink milk, pour it on cereal, cook with it. Dry milk, too, in casseroles and bakings. Add cottage cheese to scrambled eggs. Shred Cheddar on casseroles, serve with fruit for dessert. Hard cook eggs for salad toppers. Use yogurt in salad dressing. And ice cream—any questions?

Rely on the staples group to stretch your meatless meals. Corn muffins, say, with Fruited Turkey Salad, page 27. Hot rice with Eggs Foo Yung, page 64. Pad the protein with soups, too. As a beverage with Cheddar Cheese Pie, page 55, why not? And make the most of multi-talented vegetables. Beans as a main dish in Country Baked Limas, page 70. Peas as an extender in Tuna and Chips, page 33. Broccoli as a side dish with Chicken à la King, page 14.

Get the idea? It's called piecing the protein together—on a shoestring. And with your ingenuity and our Meatless Main Dishes, we predict that you will make going meatless a pleasure.

protein punchers

MILK & FRIENDS	Amount	Grams
Beverages, toppers, cooking ingredients, desserts—you name it!		
Milk (whole, non fat, buttermilk or reconstituted dry)	1 cup	9
Cottage cheese	1/4 cup	8
Cheese: Swiss	1 oz.	8
Cheddar or American process	1 oz.	7
Egg	1	6
Yogurt	1/2 cup	4
Ice cream or ice milk	1/2 cup	3

VERSATILE VEGETABLES	Amount	Grams
Side dishes. Use in salads, soups, stews or casseroles.		
Beans, lima or kidney	1/2 cup cooked	7
Green peas	1/2 cup cooked	4
Corn	1/2 cup cooked	3
Broccoli, Brussels sprouts or spinach	1/2 cup cooked	3
Potato, white or sweet	1	3
Winter squash, mashed	1/2 cup	2

SOUP DU JOUR	Amount	Grams
With meals, between meals. For beverages, snacks, lunch boxes.		
Oyster stew made with milk	1 cup	10
Split pea soup made with water	1 cup	9
Canned cream soup made with milk	1 cup	7

STAPLES & STRETCHERS	Amount	Grams
Supper stretchers for stews and casseroles. Mealtime accompaniments.		
Barley or bulgur	1/2 cup cooked	4
Corn muffin	1 med.	3
Egg noodles	1/2 cup cooked	3
Bread: Boston brown or whole wheat	1 slice	3
Cracked wheat, raisin, rye, white	1 slice	2
Rice or spaghetti	1/2 cup cooked	2
Baking powder biscuit	1 med.	2

SUPER TOPPERS	Amount	Grams
Try peanut butter on celery. Salty nuts on salads, protein chips on casseroles.		
Peanut butter	2 tbsp.	8
Chocolate-covered peanuts	1 oz.	5
Vegetable protein chips	1 tbsp.	4
Nuts: almonds, cashews, walnuts, peanuts	1 tbsp.	2

DESSERTS & SNACKS	Amount	Grams
Mealtime finales, snacktime surprises. See the milk group, too!		
Baked custard	1/2 cup	7
Pie: Pumpkin	1 piece	5
Boston Cream or lemon meringue	1 piece	4
Pudding made with milk	1/2 cup	4
Gingerbread	1 piece	2

chicken & turkey

The well-bred birds are the two best friends a meatless meal planner ever had. They'll do just about anything for you— convert to chow mein or à la king. Become a quick salad or a hearty casserole. Make a big splash as Sweet-Sour Chicken or Classic Turkey Divan. And as a final gesture, give their last protein tidbits for a homey soup or savory stew. You'll find old favorites and new in this happy collection of recipes. And the price is always right.

BREAST OF CHICKEN ON RICE

1 can (10¾ ounces) condensed cream of mushroom soup
1 soup can milk
¾ cup uncooked regular rice
1 can (4 ounces) mushroom stems and pieces
1 envelope (about 1½ ounces) onion soup mix
2 chicken breasts, split

Heat oven to 350°. Mix mushroom soup and milk; reserve ½ cup. Mix remaining soup mixture, the rice, mushrooms (with liquid) and half of the onion soup mix.

Pour into ungreased baking dish, 11¾ × 7½ × 1¾ inches. Place chicken breasts on top. Pour reserved soup mixture over chicken breasts; sprinkle with remaining onion soup mix. Cover with aluminum foil. Bake 1 hour. Uncover; bake 15 minutes longer.

4 servings/about 20 grams protein per serving.

CHICKEN OF SIX SEASONINGS

¼ cup all-purpose flour
1 teaspoon salt
½ teaspoon parsley flakes
¼ teaspoon pepper
¼ teaspoon thyme leaves
¼ teaspoon rosemary leaves
¼ teaspoon oregano leaves
¼ cup shortening
2½- to 3-pound broiler-fryer chicken,
    cut up
⅓ cup chopped onion
1 can (4 ounces) mushroom stems and
    pieces, drained (reserve liquid)
1 tablespoon brown sugar
1 tablespoon lemon juice
1 can (16 ounces) tomatoes
1 teaspoon salt
¾ cup uncooked regular rice

Mix flour, 1 teaspoon salt, the parsley flakes, pepper, thyme, rosemary and oregano leaves. Melt shortening in large skillet. Coat chicken pieces with flour mixture; reserve remaining flour mixture. Cook chicken in shortening over medium heat until light brown, 15 to 20 minutes. Remove chicken; set aside.

Add onion and mushrooms to skillet. Cook and stir until onion is tender. Stir in reserved flour mixture. Add mushroom liquid, sugar, lemon juice, tomatoes, 1 teaspoon salt and the rice.

Heat to boiling, stirring constantly; reduce heat. Add chicken; cover and simmer until rice is done and chicken is fork-tender, about 40 minutes.

6 servings/about 20 grams protein per serving.

COUNTRY CAPTAIN

½ cup all-purpose flour
1 teaspoon salt
½ teaspoon paprika
¼ teaspoon cayenne red pepper
¼ cup shortening
2½- to 3-pound broiler-fryer chicken,
    cut up
1 onion, chopped
1 clove garlic, finely chopped
1 cup water
1 can (20 ounces) tomatoes
1 teaspoon salt
1 teaspoon curry powder (optional)
½ teaspoon parsley flakes
½ teaspoon thyme
¼ teaspoon pepper
½ cup toasted slivered almonds
3 cups hot cooked rice

Mix flour, 1 teaspoon salt, the paprika and cayenne pepper. Melt shortening in large skillet. Coat chicken pieces with flour mixture. Cook chicken in shortening over medium heat until light brown, 15 to 20 minutes. Remove chicken; set aside.

Add onion and garlic to skillet. Cook and stir until onion is tender. Pour off excess fat. Stir in water, tomatoes, 1 teaspoon salt, the curry powder, parsley flakes, thyme and pepper; add the chicken pieces. Heat to boiling. Reduce heat; cover and simmer until thickest pieces are fork-tender, 30 to 45 minutes. Uncover last 10 minutes of cooking.

Place chicken on platter. Stir almonds into sauce. Spoon rice around chicken. Pour some sauce over rice; pass remainder.

6 servings/about 24 grams protein per serving.

MAI KAI CHICKEN

1 can (20 ounces) sliced pineapple
¼ cup soy sauce
2 teaspoons ginger
¼ teaspoon pepper
2½- to 3-pound broiler-fryer chicken,
    cut up
½ cup all-purpose flour
¼ cup shortening
3 cups cooked rice
¾ cup raisins
¼ cup roasted diced almonds
Curry Sauce (right)

Drain pineapple slices, reserving ⅓ cup syrup. Blend reserved pineapple syrup, the soy sauce, ginger and pepper. Place chicken pieces in large dish; pour pineapple syrup mixture over pieces. Refrigerate about 1 hour.

Turn chicken pieces and refrigerate 1 hour longer. Remove chicken and reserve pineapple syrup mixture.

Coat chicken with flour. Melt shortening in large skillet. Add chicken; cook until brown, about 20 minutes.

Heat oven to 350°. Mix rice, raisins and almonds in ungreased baking dish, 11¾ × 7½ × 1¾ inches. Place pineapple slices on rice mixture. Top with browned chicken; drizzle chicken with 3 tablespoons of the reserved syrup mixture.

Cover with aluminum foil; bake 40 minutes. Remove foil and bake until chicken is done, about 10 minutes. Serve with hot Curry Sauce.

6 servings/about 35 grams protein per serving.

CURRY SAUCE

1 tablespoon butter or margarine
1 tablespoon flour
1 tablespoon instant minced onion
½ teaspoon curry powder
¼ teaspoon ginger
⅛ teaspoon garlic powder
1 cup milk
¼ cup toasted shredded coconut

Melt butter over low heat in saucepan. Stir in flour, onion, curry powder, ginger and garlic powder. Cook, stirring constantly, until mixture is bubbly. Remove from heat; stir in milk. Heat to boiling, stirring constantly. Boil and stir 1 minute. Stir in coconut; heat through.

WHICH CHICKEN TO BUY?

The broiler-fryer is a young bird, about 9 weeks old, that weighs from 1½ to 3 pounds. But don't be misled by its name. It's your all-purpose choice and can be roasted or stewed as successfully as broiled or fried. The stewing chicken, or hen, is a plump, meaty bird, about 1½ years old, 2½ to 5 pounds in weight. It provides a generous amount of meat and is considered more flavorful than the broiler-fryer. It is also tougher and therefore does best in soups and stews.

Watch for specials on both these birds, then buy for now and for the freezer. And remember—it only takes a little extra effort to put in a second bird to roast or stew for another day.

STEWED CHICKEN

4- to 5-pound stewing chicken, cut up
1 sprig parsley
1 celery stalk with leaves, cut up
1 carrot, sliced
1 small onion, sliced
2 teaspoons salt
½ teaspoon pepper

Wash chicken; remove any excess pieces of fat. Place chicken with giblets and neck in kettle. Add enough water to just cover chicken. Add parsley, celery, carrot, onion, salt and pepper. Heat to boiling. Reduce heat; cover and simmer until thickest pieces are fork-tender, 2½ to 3½ hours. If not serving immediately, refrigerate and allow chicken to cool in broth.

Remove bones and skin from chicken; cut chicken into pieces. Skim fat from broth. Refrigerate broth and chicken pieces separately in covered containers; use within several days.

To freeze chicken pieces, pack tightly into pint freezer containers. Freeze up to one month. For longer storage, freeze chicken pieces and broth together in pint freezer containers. For best quality, use within 6 months.

4 to 5 cups cut-up cooked chicken and 5 to 6 cups broth.

Note: To stew a broiler-fryer chicken, select 3- to 4-pound broiler-fryer chicken and simmer until thickest pieces are tender, about 45 minutes.

3 to 4 cups cut-up cooked chicken and 2 to 3½ cups broth.

SWEET-SOUR CHICKEN

1 egg
2½ cups cut-up cooked chicken
¼ cup cornstarch
2 tablespoons shortening
1 can (13¼ ounces) pineapple chunks, drained (reserve syrup)
½ cup sugar
½ cup vinegar
1 medium green pepper, cut into 1-inch squares
¼ cup water
2 tablespoons cornstarch
1 teaspoon soy sauce
1 can (16 ounces) small carrots, drained
2 cups hot cooked rice

Beat egg in medium bowl. Add chicken and toss until all pieces are coated. Sprinkle ¼ cup cornstarch over chicken; toss until all pieces are well coated.

Melt shortening in 10-inch skillet. Add chicken pieces; cook over medium heat until pieces are brown on all sides. Remove pieces from skillet. Measure reserved pineapple syrup and add water to measure 1 cup. Stir liquid, sugar and vinegar into skillet. Heat to boiling, stirring constantly. Stir in green pepper; heat to boiling. Reduce heat; cover and simmer 2 minutes.

Blend water and 2 tablespoons cornstarch. Stir into skillet. Cook, stirring constantly, until mixture thickens and boils. Boil and stir 1 minute. Stir in pineapple chunks, soy sauce, carrots and chicken; heat through. Serve over rice.

4 servings/about 31 grams protein per serving.

LULANI CHICKEN

⅓ cup butter or margarine
⅓ cup all-purpose flour
½ teaspoon salt
¼ teaspoon pepper
1¾ cups chicken bouillon
⅔ cup light cream or milk
2 cups cut-up cooked chicken or turkey
¼ cup sliced water chestnuts
2 tablespoons thinly sliced green pepper
2 tablespoons thinly sliced pimiento
Rice Ring (below)

Melt butter in saucepan over low heat. Blend in flour and seasonings. Cook over low heat, stirring constantly, until mixture is smooth and bubbly. Remove from heat; stir in bouillon and cream. Heat to boiling, stirring constantly. Boil and stir 1 minute. Stir in chicken, water chestnuts, green pepper and pimiento; heat through.

Invert Rice Ring on platter. Fill with chicken mixture. If desired, garnish with pineapple.

6 servings/about 21 grams protein per serving.

RICE RING

2 cups uncooked regular rice
4 cups water
2 teaspoons salt
½ cup toasted slivered almonds
¼ cup snipped parsley

Heat rice, water and salt to boiling, stirring once or twice. Reduce heat; cover tightly and simmer 14 minutes. (Do not lift cover or stir.) Remove from heat. Fluff rice lightly with fork; cover and let steam 5 to 10 minutes. Stir in almonds and parsley. Lightly press in well-buttered 6-cup ring mold. Keep hot until serving time.

CHICKEN CHOW MEIN

2 tablespoons butter or margarine
¼ cup chopped onion
1 can (4 ounces) mushroom stems and pieces, drained (reserve liquid)
2 cups diagonally sliced celery
1 can (16 ounces) bean sprouts, drained
1 tablespoon sugar
3 tablespoons soy sauce
½ teaspoon salt
2 tablespoons cornstarch
3 tablespoons water
1½ cups cut-up cooked chicken or turkey
1 can (5 ounces) water chestnuts, thinly sliced (optional)
Chow mein noodles

Melt butter in large skillet. Add onion and mushrooms; cook and stir until onion is tender. Measure reserved mushroom liquid and add water to measure 1½ cups. Stir mushroom liquid, celery, bean sprouts, sugar, soy sauce and salt into mushroom mixture. Heat to boiling. Reduce heat; simmer uncovered 15 minutes.

Blend cornstarch and water; stir into vegetable mixture. Cook, stirring constantly, until mixture thickens and boils. Boil and stir 1 minute. Stir in chicken and water chestnuts; heat through. Serve over chow mein noodles.

4 servings/about 22 grams protein per serving.

CHICKEN MADRAS

¼ cup butter or margarine
2 small onions, chopped
1 clove garlic, finely chopped
1 stalk celery, diced
1 cup diced cooked carrots
1 tart apple, pared and diced
2 tablespoons flour
1 teaspoon curry powder
1 teaspoon salt
½ teaspoon dry mustard
⅛ teaspoon sage
1½ cups chicken bouillon
1 bay leaf
3 cups cut-up cooked chicken or turkey
½ cup light cream
2 tablespoons chopped chutney
3 cups hot cooked rice

Melt butter in 3-quart saucepan. Add onions, garlic, celery, carrots and apple; cook and stir 5 minutes. Remove from heat. Mix in flour, curry powder, salt, mustard and sage. Cook over low heat, stirring constantly, until mixture is bubbly. Remove from heat; stir in bouillon. Add bay leaf. Heat to boiling, stirring constantly. Boil and stir 1 minute. Stir in chicken, cream and chutney; heat through. Remove bay leaf.

Lightly press rice in well-buttered 4-cup ring mold. Keep hot until serving time. Invert ring on platter. Fill center with chicken mixture.

6 servings/about 24 grams protein per serving.

CAN-OPENER COMBO

1 can (16 ounces) French-style green beans, drained
1 can (10¾ ounces) condensed cream of mushroom soup
2 cans (5½ ounces each) boned chicken or 1½ cups cut-up cooked chicken or turkey
½ teaspoon sage
Chow mein noodles

Heat beans, soup, chicken and sage, stirring occasionally. Serve over noodles.

4 servings/about 20 grams protein per serving.

CHICKEN ALMOND

2 tablespoons butter or margarine
1 medium onion, sliced
¾ cup diagonally sliced celery
2 cups cut-up cooked chicken or turkey
1 can (3 ounces) sliced mushrooms
1 tablespoon cornstarch
3 tablespoons soy sauce
1 cup chicken bouillon
½ cup toasted whole almonds
3 cups hot cooked rice

Melt butter in saucepan. Add onion and celery; cook and stir until tender. Stir in chicken and mushrooms (with liquid); heat through. Blend cornstarch, soy sauce and bouillon; stir into chicken mixture. Cook, stirring constantly, until mixture thickens and boils. Boil and stir 1 minute. Stir in almonds. Serve over rice.

6 servings/about 22 grams protein per serving.

CHICKEN A LA KING

½ cup butter or margarine
1 can (4 ounces) mushroom stems and
   pieces, drained (reserve ¼ cup liquid)
½ cup chopped green pepper
½ cup all-purpose flour
1 teaspoon salt
¼ teaspoon pepper
1¾ cups chicken bouillon
2 cups milk or light cream
2 cups cut-up cooked chicken or turkey
1 cup cooked peas
2 hard-cooked eggs, cut up
1 jar (4 ounces) pimiento, chopped
8 slices toast or
   4 cups chow mein noodles

Melt butter in large skillet. Add mushrooms and green pepper; cook and stir 5 minutes. Remove from heat. Blend in flour and seasonings. Cook over low heat, stirring constantly, until mixture is bubbly. Remove from heat; stir in bouillon, milk and reserved mushroom liquid. Heat to boiling, stirring constantly. Boil and stir 1 minute. Stir in chicken, peas, eggs and pimiento; heat through. Serve over toast.

8 servings/about 19 grams protein per serving.

Note: Chicken à la King is pictured on the front cover—top row, at left.

CHEESY CHICKEN A LA KING

1 can (11 ounces) condensed Cheddar
   cheese soup
⅓ cup milk
1 cup cut-up cooked chicken or turkey
1 tablespoon chopped pimiento
2 tablespoons snipped parsley
Salt and pepper
3 slices toast

Heat soup and milk over medium heat, stirring frequently. Stir in chicken, pimiento and parsley; heat through. Season with salt and pepper. Serve over toast.

3 servings/about 20 grams protein per serving.

SPEEDY CHICKEN AND SHRIMP

3 tablespoons butter or margarine
1 medium onion, chopped
1 can (8½ ounces) pineapple tidbits,
   drained
2 cans (10½ ounces each) chicken à la king
1 can (4½ ounces) shrimp, rinsed and
   drained
2 tablespoons lemon juice
3 cups hot cooked rice
About 2 tablespoons bacon-flavored
   vegetable protein chips

Melt butter in large skillet. Add onion and pineapple; cook and stir until onion is tender. Stir in chicken à la king, shrimp and lemon juice; heat through. Serve over rice; sprinkle with protein chips.

6 servings/about 20 grams protein per serving.

CHICKEN TETRAZZINI

7 ounces uncooked spaghetti, broken
  into small pieces
¼ cup butter or margarine
¼ cup all-purpose flour
½ teaspoon salt
¼ teaspoon pepper
1 cup chicken bouillon
1 cup whipping cream
2 tablespoons sherry
2 cups cut-up cooked chicken
1 can (3 ounces) sliced mushrooms,
  drained
½ cup grated Parmesan cheese

Heat oven to 350°. Cook spaghetti as directed on package; drain.

Melt butter in large saucepan over low heat. Blend in flour and seasonings. Cook over low heat, stirring constantly, until mixture is smooth and bubbly. Remove from heat; stir in bouillon and cream. Heat to boiling, stirring constantly. Boil and stir 1 minute. Stir in sherry, spaghetti, chicken and mushrooms.

Pour into ungreased 2-quart casserole. Sprinkle with cheese. Bake until bubbly in center, about 30 minutes. Brown top by placing briefly under broiler. If desired, garnish with parsley and sliced green olives.

6 servings/about 25 grams protein per serving.

Note: Chicken Tetrazzini is pictured on the back cover—top row, at left.

CHICKEN CARUSO

About 2 cups uncooked elbow macaroni
  (7 or 8 ounces)
4 cups chicken bouillon
2 tablespoons butter or margarine
½ cup finely chopped green pepper
⅓ cup finely chopped onion
2 cups cut-up cooked chicken or turkey
2 cups shredded process American
  cheese (about 8 ounces)
¼ cup chopped pimiento
¼ cup toasted slivered almonds
1 package (10 ounces) frozen green peas,
  cooked and drained
3 tablespoons sherry

Boil macaroni in bouillon 10 minutes or until tender; do not drain. Melt butter in large skillet. Add green pepper and onion; cook and stir until onion is just tender. Stir in chicken, cheese, pimiento, almonds, peas, sherry and cooked macaroni (with bouillon); heat through. If desired, garnish with tomato slices and parsley.

8 servings/about 24 grams protein per serving.

STORING FRESH POULTRY

When you get the bird home, loosen the plastic wrap and store in coldest part of refrigerator. Use in 1 or 2 days. To freeze fresh poultry—wash, pat dry and wrap tightly in moisture-vaporproof wrap. (Store giblets separately.) Use in 2 to 3 months. Note! Supermarket tray packs can be frozen, but only up to 2 weeks.

CHICKEN-MUSHROOM SQUARES

3 cups soft bread crumbs (about 4 slices
   bread)
3 cups cut-up cooked chicken or turkey
1 cup chicken bouillon
1 cup milk
1 can (4 ounces) sliced mushrooms,
   drained
2 eggs, beaten
¼ cup chopped pimiento
2 tablespoons chopped onion
1 teaspoon salt
⅛ teaspoon pepper
Mushroom Sauce (below)

Heat oven to 350°. Mix all ingredients except sauce. Pour into ungreased baking dish, 11¾ × 7½ × 1¾ inches. Place baking dish in pan of hot water (1 inch deep).

Bake uncovered until knife inserted 1 inch from edge comes out clean, 1 to 1¼ hours. Cut into squares and serve with sauce or, if desired, garnish with parsley.

8 servings/about 20 grams protein per serving.

MUSHROOM SAUCE

2 tablespoons butter or margarine
1 thin slice onion
1 cup sliced fresh mushrooms or 1 can
   (2 ounces) sliced mushrooms, drained
2 tablespoons flour
1 cup beef bouillon
¼ teaspoon salt
⅛ teaspoon pepper
Few drops Worcestershire sauce

Melt butter in skillet over low heat until golden brown. Add onion; cook and stir until tender. Discard onion. Stir mushrooms into melted butter; brown slowly. Blend in flour. Cook over low heat, stirring constantly, until flour is deep brown. Remove from heat; stir in bouillon. Heat to boiling, stirring constantly. Boil and stir 1 minute. Stir in salt, pepper and Worcestershire sauce.

CHILI-CHICKEN CASSEROLE

16 ounces uncooked medium egg noodles
2 tablespoons butter or margarine
1 medium onion, chopped
3 cans (10¾ ounces each) condensed
   cream of mushroom soup
1 can (4 ounces) pimiento, chopped
2 tablespoons finely chopped pickled
   hot green chilies (remove stems
   and seeds)
3 to 4 cups cut-up cooked chicken or
   turkey
Salt and pepper
2 to 3 cups shredded sharp Cheddar
   cheese (8 to 12 ounces)

Heat oven to 350°. Cook noodles as directed on package; drain.

Melt butter in large skillet. Add onion; cook and stir until tender. Stir in soup, pimiento and chilies.

Layer half of the noodles and half of the chicken in greased 4-quart casserole; season with salt and pepper. Top with half of the soup mixture and half of the cheese. Repeat layers. Bake uncovered about 45 minutes.

12 servings/about 24 grams protein per serving.

CHICKEN-RICE CASSEROLE

¼ cup butter or margarine
⅓ cup all-purpose flour
1½ teaspoons salt
⅛ teaspoon pepper
1 cup chicken bouillon
1½ cups milk
1½ cups cooked white or wild rice
2 cups cut-up cooked chicken
1 can (3 ounces) sliced mushrooms,
   drained
⅓ cup chopped green pepper
2 tablespoons chopped pimiento
¼ cup slivered almonds

Heat oven to 350°. Melt butter in sauce-pan. Blend in flour and seasonings. Cook over low heat, stirring constantly, until mixture is smooth and bubbly. Remove from heat; stir in bouillon and milk. Heat to boiling, stirring constantly. Boil and stir 1 minute. Stir in remaining ingredients.

Pour into ungreased baking dish, 10 × 6 × 1½ inches, or 1½-quart casserole. Bake uncovered 40 to 45 minutes. If desired, sprinkle with snipped parsley.

6 servings/about 20 grams protein per serving.

CHICKEN-ASPARAGUS-CHEESE BAKE

1 package (10 ounces) frozen cut
   asparagus, cooked and drained
6 slices cooked chicken or turkey
½ teaspoon marjoram
½ teaspoon sage
2 eggs, beaten
½ cup milk
1 cup shredded process American cheese
   (about 4 ounces)
1 cup all-purpose flour*
2 teaspoons baking powder
1 teaspoon salt
Cheese Sauce (below)

Heat oven to 350°. Line ungreased baking dish, 11¾ × 7½ × 1¾ inches, with layer of cooked asparagus. Place chicken slices on asparagus. Sprinkle marjoram and sage over chicken.

Mix eggs, milk and cheese; stir in flour, baking powder and salt. Spread egg mixture evenly over chicken.

Bake uncovered until golden brown, 25 to 30 minutes. Cut into squares; serve hot with Cheese Sauce.

8 servings/about 19 grams protein per serving.

* If using self-rising flour, omit baking powder and salt.

CHEESE SAUCE

1 can (11 ounces) condensed Cheddar
   cheese soup
⅓ cup milk
¼ teaspoon dry mustard
¼ teaspoon Worcestershire sauce

Heat all ingredients just to boiling, stirring frequently.

CHICKEN-MACARONI CASSEROLE

1½ cups uncooked elbow macaroni
   (5 ounces)
1 cup shredded Cheddar cheese (about 4
   ounces)
1½ cups cut-up cooked chicken
1 can (4 ounces) mushroom stems and
   pieces, drained
¼ cup chopped pimiento
1 can (10¾ ounces) condensed cream of
   chicken soup
1 cup milk
½ teaspoon salt
½ teaspoon curry powder

Heat oven to 350°. Stir together all ingredients. Pour into ungreased 1½-quart casserole. Cover; bake 1 hour.

6 servings/about 21 grams protein per serving.

CHICKEN POT PIE

⅓ cup butter or margarine
⅓ cup all-purpose flour*
⅓ cup chopped onion
½ teaspoon salt
¼ teaspoon pepper
1¾ cups chicken bouillon
⅔ cup milk
2 cups cut-up cooked chicken or turkey
1 package (10 ounces) frozen peas and
   carrots
Celery Seed Pastry (right)

Heat oven to 425°. Melt butter in saucepan over low heat. Blend in flour, onion and seasonings. Cook over low heat, stirring constantly, until mixture is bubbly. Remove from heat; stir in bouillon and milk. Heat to boiling, stirring constantly. Boil and stir 1 minute. Gently stir in chicken and frozen vegetables; set aside.

Prepare pastry. Roll ⅔ of pastry on lightly floured cloth-covered board into 13-inch square. Ease pastry into square pan, 9 × 9 × 2 inches; pour chicken filling into pastry-lined pan. Roll remaining pastry into 11-inch square; place over filling. Roll edges under; flute. Cut slits in center to allow steam to escape. Bake 30 to 35 minutes.

5 servings/about 26 grams protein per serving.

* If using self-rising flour, omit salt.

CELERY SEED PASTRY

2 cups all-purpose flour**
2 teaspoons celery seed
1 teaspoon salt
⅔ cup plus 2 tablespoons shortening
4 to 5 tablespoons cold water

Measure flour, celery seed and salt into bowl. Cut in shortening thoroughly. Sprinkle with water, 1 tablespoon at a time, mixing until flour is moistened and pastry almost cleans side of bowl. Gather into ball.

** If using self-rising flour, omit salt. Pastry made with self-rising flour differs in flavor and texture.

GOURMET CHICKEN LIVERS

2 cups boiling water
½ cup wild rice
2 tablespoons butter or margarine
¼ pound fresh mushrooms, sliced
¾ cup chopped onion
½ cup chopped celery
2 cans (13¾ ounces each) condensed chicken broth
½ cup uncooked long-grain rice
½ teaspoon salt
¼ teaspoon thyme
⅛ teaspoon pepper
1 pound chicken livers
¼ cup all-purpose flour
2 tablespoons butter or margarine
¼ cup snipped parsley
2 tablespoons bacon-flavored vegetable protein chips

Pour boiling water over wild rice. Cover; let stand 20 minutes. Heat oven to 350°. Melt 2 tablespoons butter in saucepan. Add mushrooms, onion and celery; cook and stir until onion is tender. Stir in broth; heat to boiling. Remove from heat.

Place wild rice, long-grain rice, salt, thyme and pepper in ungreased 2-quart casserole. Stir in chicken broth mixture. Cover and bake 30 minutes.

Coat chicken livers with flour. Melt 2 tablespoons butter in skillet. Add livers; cook and stir until brown, 3 to 4 minutes.

Remove casserole from oven; stir in parsley. Arrange livers around edge of dish. Cover and bake until rice is cooked, about 30 minutes. Sprinkle with protein chips.

6 servings/about 20 grams protein per serving.

MULLIGATAWNY SOUP

3- to 4-pound broiler-fryer chicken, cut up
1 quart water
1 tablespoon salt
1 teaspoon curry powder
⅛ teaspoon mace
⅛ teaspoon cloves
1 small bunch parsley
¼ cup butter or margarine
1 medium onion, sliced
1 medium carrot, sliced
1 stalk celery, sliced
1 green pepper, diced
1 medium apple, pared and sliced
⅓ cup all-purpose flour
1 can (8 ounces) stewed tomatoes

Combine chicken, water, salt, curry powder, mace, cloves and parsley. Heat to boiling. Reduce heat; cover and simmer until chicken is tender, about 45 minutes.

Remove chicken from broth. Measure broth; if necessary, add water to measure 1 quart. Remove bones and skin from chicken; cut chicken into pieces.

Melt butter in large saucepan. Add onion, carrot, celery, green pepper and apple; cook and stir until tender. Remove from heat; stir in flour. Gradually stir in broth and tomatoes; add chicken. Heat to boiling, stirring constantly. Boil and stir 1 minute. Reduce heat; cover and simmer 1 hour.

8 servings, 1½ cups each/about 16 grams protein per serving.

CHICKEN-SHRIMP GUMBO

4-pound stewing chicken, cut up
2 teaspoons salt
2 tablespoons shortening
2½ cups cold water
⅓ cup all-purpose flour
2 cups chopped onion
1 can (16 ounces) tomatoes
1 can (6 ounces) tomato paste
1 package (10 ounces) frozen corn,
   broken apart
1 tablespoon sugar
1 tablespoon Worcestershire sauce
1 teaspoon salt
1 teaspoon thyme leaves
¼ teaspoon cayenne red pepper
2 bay leaves
1 clove garlic, finely chopped
1 can (16 ounces) cut okra, drained
14 to 16 ounces cleaned raw shrimp,
   fresh or frozen
3 cups hot cooked rice

Sprinkle chicken pieces with 2 teaspoons salt. Melt shortening in large kettle; add chicken pieces. Cook until brown. Remove chicken; drain. Drain fat from kettle.

Mix water and flour; pour into kettle. Heat to boiling, stirring constantly. Stir in onion, tomatoes, tomato paste, corn, sugar, Worcestershire sauce, 1 teaspoon salt, the thyme leaves, cayenne pepper, bay leaves and garlic; add chicken pieces. Heat to boiling. Reduce heat; cover and simmer 2 hours. Stir occasionally and skim off excess fat.

Stir in okra; simmer uncovered until chicken is tender, about 1 hour. Stir in shrimp; cook until shrimp are pink, 10 to 20 minutes. Do not overcook shrimp. Remove from heat. Lift out bay leaves. (If desired, stir ¼ teaspoon gumbo filé powder into each serving. Gumbo filé powder will thicken mixture slightly.)

Place scoop of rice in each soup plate. Fill with gumbo; then add 1 or 2 pieces of chicken.

10 servings/about 25 grams protein per serving.

EASY CHICKEN GUMBO

3 tablespoons butter or margarine
1 can (16 ounces) cut okra, drained
¼ cup chopped onion
¼ cup chopped green pepper
4 cups chicken bouillon
1 can (16 ounces) tomatoes
1 small bay leaf
1 teaspoon salt
Dash of pepper
2 cups cut-up cooked chicken or turkey
1 tablespoon snipped parsley
3 cups hot cooked rice

Melt butter in large saucepan. Add okra, onion and green pepper; cook and stir until onion is tender. Stir in bouillon, tomatoes, bay leaf, salt and pepper. Heat to boiling. Reduce heat; simmer 15 minutes. Stir in chicken and parsley; heat through. Place scoop of rice in each bowl; top with chicken mixture.

6 servings/about 17 grams protein per serving.

Note: Easy Chicken Gumbo is pictured on the front cover—top row, at right.

CHICKEN PROVINCIAL

Two 2½-pound broiler-fryer chickens,
  cut up
1 tablespoon plus 1 teaspoon seasoned
  salt
½ teaspoon seasoned pepper
½ teaspoon paprika
3½ cups water
6 carrots, halved
6 small potatoes, pared
6 small onions
1½ teaspoons parsley flakes
French bread or hard rolls

Wash chickens. Place chickens, seasoned salt, seasoned pepper, paprika and water in large kettle. Heat to boiling. Reduce heat; cover and simmer 1 hour. Add vegetables and, if necessary, more water. Cover and cook until vegetables are tender, about 40 minutes.

Skim fat from broth. Divide chicken, vegetables and broth among 6 soup bowls; sprinkle each with ¼ teaspoon parsley flakes. Serve with French bread.

6 servings/about 36 grams protein per serving.

Note: Chicken Provincial is pictured on the front cover—bottom row, center.

PEANUT CHICKEN STEW

2 tablespoons shortening
2 green peppers, cut into rings
1 medium onion, cut into rings
1 can (6 ounces) tomato paste
¾ cup peanut butter
3 cups chicken bouillon
1½ teaspoons salt
1 teaspoon sugar
1 teaspoon chili powder
½ teaspoon nutmeg
4 cups cut-up cooked chicken
4 cups hot cooked rice
Accompaniments (below)

Melt shortening in large skillet. Add peppers and onion; cook until onion is tender. Drain off excess fat.

Blend tomato paste and peanut butter; stir in bouillon and seasonings. Add peanut butter mixture and chicken to skillet; cook and stir over low heat until heated through. (If stew is too thick, stir in additional chicken bouillon.) Serve over hot rice with the Accompaniments (some or all may be used).

8 servings/about 30 grams protein per serving.

ACCOMPANIMENTS
Chopped green pepper
Grated coconut
Sautéed banana slices (¼ inch thick)
Coarsely ground or chopped peanuts
Sautéed onion slices
Sautéed tomato slices
Sautéed eggplant slices
Pineapple cubes
Raisins

CHICKEN PARAGON SALAD

3 tablespoons lemon juice
2½ cups cut-up cooked chicken or turkey
1 teaspoon salt
½ teaspoon monosodium glutamate
¼ teaspoon sage
⅛ teaspoon pepper
1½ cups water
2 chicken bouillon cubes
¾ cup uncooked regular rice
½ cup chopped green pepper
¼ cup diced celery
¼ cup sliced green onions (with tops)
1 jar (2 ounces) pimiento, chopped
⅓ cup toasted slivered almonds
¾ cup mayonnaise or salad dressing
3 tablespoons milk
1 package (10 ounces) frozen green
   peas, cooked, drained and cooled
Lettuce cups

Drizzle lemon juice over chicken. Sprinkle with seasonings and toss. Cover and refrigerate at least 4 hours.

Heat water, bouillon cubes and rice in large saucepan to boiling, stirring once or twice. Reduce heat; cover tightly and simmer 14 minutes or until rice is tender and all liquid is absorbed. Remove from heat. Fluff lightly with a fork; cover and let stand 10 minutes. Spread rice on baking sheet; cover with plastic wrap and chill thoroughly.

Mix chicken (with marinade), green pepper, celery, onions, pimiento, almonds and chilled rice. Blend mayonnaise and milk; fold into chicken mixture. Gently stir in peas. Cover and refrigerate at least 1 hour. Serve in lettuce cups.

9 servings/about 16 grams protein per serving.

CHICKEN-MACARONI SALAD

1 cup uncooked elbow macaroni
   (4 ounces)
1 cup diced cucumber
2 cups cut-up cooked chicken or turkey
1 tablespoon finely chopped onion
1 tablespoon snipped parsley or 1
   teaspoon parsley flakes
¾ cup mayonnaise or salad dressing
½ teaspoon salt
¼ teaspoon pepper
4 cups bite-size pieces lettuce

Cook macaroni as directed on package; drain and rinse in cold water.

Mix all ingredients except lettuce. Cover and refrigerate.

Just before serving, toss chicken mixture with lettuce. If desired, garnish with parsleyed tomato wedges.

6 servings/about 16 grams protein per serving.

VARIATIONS

Salmon-Macaroni Salad: Substitute 1 can (16 ounces) salmon, drained, skinned and boned, for the chicken.

About 17 grams protein per serving.

Tuna-Macaroni Salad: Substitute 1 can (9¾ ounces) tuna, drained, for the chicken.

About 22 grams protein per serving.

SMOKED TURKEY ROYALE

1 package (10 ounces) frozen chopped broccoli
¼ cup butter or margarine
¼ cup all-purpose flour
¼ teaspoon pepper
¼ teaspoon sage
¾ cup light cream
1 can (13¾ ounces) condensed chicken broth
2 packages (3 ounces each) sliced smoked turkey, cut up
½ cup shredded Cheddar cheese
3 cups hot cooked rice

Cook broccoli as directed on package; drain.

Melt butter in skillet over low heat. Blend in flour and seasonings. Cook over low heat, stirring constantly, until mixture is smooth and bubbly. Remove from heat; stir in cream and broth. Heat to boiling, stirring constantly. Boil and stir 1 minute. Stir in broccoli and turkey; heat through. Sprinkle cheese on top; cover until cheese is melted. Serve over rice.

6 servings/about 16 grams protein per serving.

STUFFED TURKEY SLICES

¼ cup butter or margarine
½ cup diced celery
½ cup chopped onion
1 egg, slightly beaten
2 cups mashed potatoes
½ cup herb-seasoned bread stuffing
¼ cup snipped parsley
½ teaspoon salt
Dash of pepper
8 to 10 large slices cooked turkey
½ cup chicken bouillon

Heat oven to 425°. Melt butter in saucepan. Add celery and onion; cook and stir until tender. Stir egg into potatoes; add stuffing, parsley, salt and pepper. Stir in celery and onion.

For each serving, cut an oval, about 13 × 7 inches, from heavy-duty aluminum foil. (Size of foil will depend on size of turkey slices.) Place slice of turkey on half of the oval. Top with some of the potato mixture. Place second turkey slice on potato mixture. Pour 2 tablespoons bouillon over turkey. Fold other half of foil over. Close and seal by folding 2 edges together (a double fold). Repeat with remaining turkey slices. Place on baking sheet.

Bake 20 to 25 minutes. Cut slits in top of foil and fold back. Serve with turkey gravy and whole cranberry sauce if desired.

5 servings/about 31 grams protein per serving.

TURKEY DINNER PIE

1 package (11 or 22 ounces) pie crust
  mix or sticks
1 can (10¾ ounces) condensed cream of
  chicken soup
2¼ cups cut-up cooked turkey or chicken
1 package (10 ounces) frozen carrots and
  peas, thawed
1 can (8 ounces) onions, halved
1 teaspoon salt
⅛ teaspoon pepper
⅛ teaspoon thyme

Heat oven to 425°. Prepare pastry for 9-inch Two-crust Pie as directed on package.

Mix remaining ingredients; turn into pastry-lined pie pan. Cover with top crust which has slits cut in it; seal and flute.

Bake until golden brown, 35 to 40 minutes.

6 servings/about 22 grams protein per serving.

TALKING TURKEY

Take your pick of fresh or quick-frozen turkey. But be aware that the big bird now comes in frozen halves and quarters— the quarters usually weighing about 6 pounds, enough to serve 8. If you can't find the frozen turkey parts, buy a whole bird and ask the meatman to cut it for you. Use some, freeze the rest. Since you can store turkey parts easily in the freezer, it's a shrewd investment. Besides, anything as good as turkey deserves to be eaten often.

CLASSIC TURKEY DIVAN

¼ cup butter or margarine
¼ cup all-purpose flour
1½ cups chicken bouillon
2 tablespoons sherry
⅛ teaspoon nutmeg
½ cup whipping cream, whipped
½ cup grated Parmesan cheese
1½ pounds fresh broccoli, cooked and
  drained, or 2 packages (10 ounces
  each) frozen broccoli spears, cooked
  and drained
5 large slices cooked turkey or chicken
  breast meat (about ¾ pound)
½ cup grated Parmesan cheese

Melt butter over low heat in medium saucepan. Blend in flour. Cook over low heat, stirring constantly, until mixture is smooth and bubbly. Remove from heat; stir in bouillon. Heat to boiling, stirring constantly. Boil and stir 1 minute. Remove from heat; stir in sherry and nutmeg. Gently fold in whipped cream and ½ cup cheese.

Place hot broccoli in ungreased baking dish, 11¾ × 7½ × 1¾ inches; top with turkey slices. Pour sauce over mixture. Sprinkle with ½ cup cheese. Set oven control at broil and/or 550°. Place baking dish under broiler with top 3 to 5 inches from heat; broil until cheese is bubbly and light brown.

5 servings/about 32 grams protein per serving.

ISLAND SKILLET DINNER

1 pound fresh green beans
½ cup water
1 teaspoon salt
1 cup sliced celery
1 medium green pepper, cut into ¼-inch strips
1 pound sliced cooked turkey or chicken
1½ cups cherry tomatoes
1 can (20 ounces) pineapple spears, drained (reserve syrup)
1 ripe banana
Oriental Sauce (right)
Hot buttered rice

Wash beans and remove ends (leave beans whole). Heat water and salt to boiling in 12- or 14-inch skillet; place beans on one side of skillet and celery and green pepper on the other side.

Cook uncovered 5 minutes. Cover tightly and cook until beans are tender, 20 to 25 minutes. (Stir in additional water, if necessary, to prevent scorching.)

Push beans into pie-shaped wedge, occupying about 1/5 of the skillet; arrange sliced turkey in wedge next to beans; arrange celery and green pepper in wedge next to turkey; arrange tomatoes in wedge next to celery and green pepper; arrange pineapple spears in wedge next to tomatoes. Slice banana over pineapple.

Pour Oriental Sauce over entire mixture. Heat to boiling. Reduce heat; cover and simmer until heated through, 10 to 15 minutes. Serve with rice.

6 servings/about 20 grams protein per serving.

ORIENTAL SAUCE

3 tablespoons cornstarch
3 tablespoons light molasses
Reserved pineapple syrup
⅓ cup vinegar
¾ cup brown sugar (packed)
¾ cup cold water
2 chicken bouillon cubes

Combine all ingredients in saucepan. Cook, stirring constantly, until mixture thickens and boils. Boil and stir 1 minute.

TURKEY AU GRATIN

¼ cup butter or margarine
¼ cup all-purpose flour
½ teaspoon salt
½ teaspoon paprika
½ teaspoon dry mustard
2¼ cups milk
½ cup shredded American cheese
2 cups cut-up cooked turkey or chicken
2 tablespoons sliced pimiento-stuffed olives
1 can (2 ounces) chopped pimiento
2 tablespoons sherry flavoring
Toast triangles

Melt butter over low heat in saucepan. Blend in flour and seasonings. Cook over low heat, stirring constantly, until mixture is smooth and bubbly. Remove from heat; stir in milk. Heat to boiling, stirring constantly. Boil and stir 1 minute. Remove from heat; stir in cheese until melted. Stir in turkey, olives, pimiento and flavoring; heat through. Serve over toast triangles.

6 servings/about 20 grams protein per serving.

TURKEY MOCK STROGANOFF

3 ounces uncooked egg noodles
¼ cup butter or margarine
1 small onion, finely chopped
1 can (6 ounces) sliced mushrooms,
 drained (reserve liquid)
2 tablespoons snipped parsley
1 can (10¾ ounces) condensed cream
 of chicken soup or cream of celery
 soup
⅓ cup milk
2½ cups cut-up cooked turkey or chicken
¼ cup sliced pimiento-stuffed olives
⅛ teaspoon thyme
Salt and pepper
2 tablespoons butter or margarine
1 cup dairy sour cream
½ cup buttered bread crumbs
¼ cup jellied cranberries

Cook egg noodles as directed on package; drain.

Melt ¼ cup butter in saucepan. Add onion and mushrooms; cook and stir until onion is tender. Stir in parsley, soup, milk and mushroom liquid. Stir in turkey, olives and seasonings; heat through.

Toss noodles with 2 tablespoons butter. Stir sour cream slowly into turkey mixture; heat through (but be sure not to let mixture come to a boil, or sour cream may curdle slightly).

Arrange noodles in a ring on large platter. Fill center with turkey mixture. Sprinkle with buttered crumbs; place mound of cranberries in center. If desired, garnish with parsley.

6 servings/about 23 grams protein per serving.

GARDEN SUPPER CASSEROLE

2 cups soft bread cubes (about 2 slices)
½ cup shredded sharp cheese
2 tablespoons butter or margarine,
 melted
1 cup cooked peas or other vegetable
3 tablespoons butter or margarine
2 tablespoons chopped onion
3 tablespoons flour
1 teaspoon salt
⅛ teaspoon pepper
1½ cups milk
1 cup cut-up cooked turkey or chicken
1 large tomato, sliced

Heat oven to 350°. Mix bread cubes, cheese and 2 tablespoons butter; spread half of the mixture in greased 1-quart casserole. Spread peas over bread mixture.

Melt 3 tablespoons butter over low heat. Add onion; cook and stir until tender. Blend in flour and seasonings. Cook over low heat, stirring constantly, until mixture is bubbly. Remove from heat; stir in milk. Heat to boiling, stirring constantly. Boil and stir 1 minute. Stir in turkey; pour sauce over peas. Arrange tomato slices over sauce and spread with remaining bread mixture. Bake uncovered 25 minutes.

4 servings/about 22 grams protein per serving.

Note: Garden Supper Casserole is pictured on the back cover—bottom row, at right.

TURKEY IN STUFFING SHELLS

2 tablespoons flour
1 teaspoon instant minced onion
¼ teaspoon salt
¼ teaspoon mace
Dash of pepper
1¼ cups light cream
2 cups cut-up cooked turkey or chicken
1 package (10 ounces) frozen green peas
    with onions, cooked and drained
2 tablespoons chopped pimiento
1 teaspoon grated lemon peel
Stuffing Shells (below)

Heat oven to 425°. Combine flour, onion and seasonings in saucepan. Gradually stir in cream. Heat to boiling, stirring constantly. Boil and stir 1 minute. Stir in turkey, peas, pimiento and lemon peel; heat through.

Pour hot mixture into Stuffing Shells. Sprinkle reserved stuffing mixture around edge of each. Bake until stuffing edge is light brown, about 5 minutes.

5 servings/about 23 grams protein per serving.

STUFFING SHELLS

1 package (8 ounces) herb-seasoned
    stuffing, crushed
½ cup butter or margarine, melted
⅓ cup water

Mix all ingredients. Reserve 1½ cups; divide remaining stuffing mixture among 5 individual pie pans or casseroles. Press mixture against bottom and side of each.

FRUITED TURKEY SALAD

1½ cups cut-up cooked turkey or chicken
1 can (8¼ ounces) green grapes, drained,
    or 1 cup fresh seedless green grapes
1 can (5 ounces) water chestnuts,
    drained and chopped
1 can (11 ounces) mandarin orange
    segments, drained
½ cup mayonnaise or salad dressing
½ teaspoon salt or 1 teaspoon soy sauce
¼ teaspoon curry powder

Combine turkey, grapes, water chestnuts and orange segments. Mix remaining ingredients; toss with turkey mixture.

4 servings/about 16 grams protein per serving.

VARIATION

Fruited Turkey-Macaroni Salad: Cook 1½ cups elbow macaroni (6 ounces) as directed on package; rinse in cold water and drain. Mix with remaining ingredients.

About 20 grams protein per serving.

fish & seafood

Can meat eaters find happiness with fish and seafood? You bet your budget! Show us the man who doesn't enjoy a Simple Saucy Fish Bake—especially when he catches the fish himself. How many youngsters do you know who wouldn't go for Tuna Pizza or Salmon Turnovers? Imagine guests unimpressed by Seafood à la Newburg or Skillet Paella. These and many other good things of the sea, represented in this chapter, could inspire a new form of cooking at your house. So introduce the family to a fish bake tonight. And plan a fishing trip soon.

TUNA-MACARONI CASSEROLE

1½ cups uncooked elbow macaroni
  (6 ounces)
1 can (6½ ounces) tuna, drained
2 cups shredded Cheddar cheese (about
  8 ounces)
1 medium onion, finely chopped
1 can (10¾ ounces) condensed cream of
  mushroom soup
1 soup can water

Heat oven to 350°. Cook macaroni as directed on package; drain.

Mix macaroni, tuna, cheese and onion. Pour into greased 2-quart casserole. Heat soup and water to boiling, stirring frequently. Pour over macaroni mixture. Bake uncovered until mixture is bubbly, 30 to 35 minutes.

6 servings/about 22 grams protein per serving.

TUNA WITH NOODLES

1 package (6 ounces) noodles almondine
1 can (6½ ounces) tuna, drained
1 package (10 ounces) frozen mixed
   vegetables, thawed, or 1 cup cooked
   mixed vegetables (peas, carrots, beans
   or corn)

Heat oven to 375°. Prepare noodles almondine as directed on package for oven method except—decrease boiling water to 2 cups. Stir in tuna and vegetables. Cover; bake 20 to 25 minutes. Stir before serving. Sprinkle with almonds.

4 servings/about 19 grams protein per serving.

Note: Tuna with Noodles is pictured on the back cover—bottom row, at left.

TUNA SCALLOP

3 tablespoons butter or margarine
3 tablespoons flour
¾ teaspoon salt
Dash of pepper
½ teaspoon dry mustard
1½ cups milk
¼ cup snipped parsley
1 cup shredded American or Cheddar
   cheese (about 4 ounces)
½ cup chopped onion
2 cups thinly sliced cooked potato
1 can (6½ ounces) tuna, drained
¼ cup buttered bread crumbs

Heat oven to 375°. Melt butter over low heat in saucepan. Blend in flour and sea-sonings. Cook over low heat, stirring constantly, until mixture is smooth and bubbly. Remove from heat; stir in milk. Heat to boiling, stirring constantly. Boil and stir 1 minute. Remove from heat; stir in parsley, cheese and onion.

Alternate layers of potato, tuna and sauce in greased 1½-quart casserole. Sprinkle with bread crumbs. Bake uncovered 40 to 45 minutes.

6 servings/about 19 grams protein per serving.

ONE-DISH TUNA AND RICE

1 egg
1½ cups uncooked instant rice
2 cups shredded process cheese (about
   8 ounces)
2 cans (6½ ounces each) tuna, drained
⅓ cup sliced pimiento-stuffed olives
2 tablespoons snipped parsley
1 tablespoon plus 1½ teaspoons instant
   minced onion or ¼ cup chopped onion
2 teaspoons dry mustard
1 teaspoon salt
Dash of pepper
1 can (13 ounces) evaporated milk
½ cup water

Heat oven to 350°. Beat egg slightly in ungreased 2-quart casserole; mix in rice, 1½ cups of the cheese, the tuna, olives and seasonings. Stir in milk and water. Sprinkle remaining cheese on top. Cover; bake 45 minutes.

8 servings/about 27 grams protein per serving.

TUNA GOURMET

8 ounces uncooked egg noodles
2 cans (6½ ounces each) tuna, well
   drained
1½ cups dairy sour cream
¾ cup milk
1 can (3 ounces) sliced mushrooms,
   drained
1½ teaspoons salt
¼ teaspoon pepper
¼ cup dry bread crumbs
¼ cup grated Parmesan cheese
2 tablespoons butter or margarine, melted
Paprika

Heat oven to 350°. Cook noodles as directed on package; drain and return to saucepan.

Stir in tuna, sour cream, milk, mushrooms, salt and pepper. Pour into ungreased 2-quart casserole. Mix bread crumbs, cheese and butter; sprinkle over casserole. Sprinkle paprika over bread crumb mixture. Bake uncovered until bubbly and heated through, 35 to 40 minutes.

8 servings/about 21 grams protein per serving.

TUNA DIVAN

1 can (15 ounces) cut asparagus
Milk
3 tablespoons butter or margarine
¼ cup all-purpose flour
1 teaspoon salt
2 cans (6½ ounces each) tuna, drained
3 cheese slices
Pimiento strips

Heat oven to 425°. Drain asparagus; add milk to asparagus liquid to measure 2 cups and set aside.

Melt butter in saucepan. Blend in flour and salt. Cook over low heat, stirring constantly, until mixture is smooth. Remove from heat; stir in asparagus liquid. Heat to boiling, stirring constantly. Boil and stir 1 minute.

Spread tuna in ungreased 1½-quart casserole. Pour half of the sauce over tuna; arrange asparagus in layer on top. Pour remaining sauce over asparagus. Garnish with cheese slices and pimiento strips. Bake uncovered until bubbly, about 15 minutes.

8 servings/about 18 grams protein per serving.

TUNA DINNER IN A DISH

4 hard-cooked eggs
1½ cups cut-up celery
1 can (6½ ounces) tuna, drained
¼ cup butter or margarine
¼ cup all-purpose flour
1½ teaspoons salt
¼ teaspoon pepper
2 cups milk
1 small onion, thinly sliced
¼ cup chopped green pepper
Cheese Crescents (below)

Heat oven to 425°. Cut peeled eggs lengthwise in half. Arrange eggs, celery and tuna in ungreased baking dish, 8 × 8 × 2 inches.

Melt butter in saucepan over low heat. Blend in flour and seasonings. Cook over low heat, stirring constantly, until mixture is smooth and bubbly. Remove from heat; stir in milk. Heat to boiling, stirring constantly. Boil and stir 1 minute. Remove from heat; stir in onion and green pepper. Pour over mixture in dish. Keep hot in oven while making Cheese Crescents. Arrange crescents on top of hot mixture. Bake uncovered 25 to 30 minutes.

6 servings/about 22 grams protein per serving.

CHEESE CRESCENTS

1 cup all-purpose flour*
1½ teaspoons baking powder
½ teaspoon salt
½ cup shredded American cheese
3 tablespoons salad oil
⅓ cup milk

Measure flour, baking powder, salt and cheese into bowl. Pour oil and milk into measuring cup (do not stir); pour all at once into flour mixture. Stir until mixture cleans side of bowl and forms a ball. Knead about 10 times. Roll into 8-inch circle between 2 sheets of waxed paper. Cut dough into 6 wedges. Roll up, beginning at rounded edge.

* If using self-rising flour, omit baking powder and salt.

Note: Tuna Dinner in a Dish is pictured on the front cover—bottom row, at right.

VARIATION

Chicken Dinner in a Dish: Substitute 2 cups cut-up cooked chicken for the tuna.

About 27 grams protein per serving.

TUNA-RICE MELANGE

1 tablespoon salad oil
1 small onion, thinly sliced
1 package (10 ounces) frozen mixed
   vegetables
½ cup water
3 cups unsalted cooked rice
2 cans (6½ ounces each) tuna, drained
1 can (5 ounces) water chestnuts, sliced
½ cup thinly sliced celery
¼ cup soy sauce

Heat oil in large skillet. Add onion; cook and stir until tender. Add frozen vegetables and water. Heat to boiling. Reduce heat; cover and simmer until vegetables are tender, 5 to 10 minutes. Stir in remaining ingredients; heat through.

6 servings/about 21 grams protein per serving.

TUNA BISCUIT RING

1 egg, slightly beaten
2 cans (6½ ounces each) tuna, drained
½ cup chopped onion
½ cup shredded sharp Cheddar cheese
½ cup snipped parsley
1 teaspoon celery salt
¼ teaspoon pepper
Biscuit Dough (below)
Cheese Sauce (page 62)

Heat oven to 375°. Reserve 2 tablespoons of the egg; set aside. Mix remaining egg, the tuna, onion, cheese, parsley, celery salt and pepper.

Prepare Biscuit Dough. Roll dough into rectangle, 15 × 10 inches; spread with tuna mixture. Roll up, beginning at wide side. Place seam side down in ring on greased baking sheet. Pinch ends together. With scissors, make cuts ⅔ of the way through ring at 1-inch intervals. Turn each section on its side; brush with reserved egg. Bake 25 to 30 minutes. Serve with hot Cheese Sauce.

8 servings/about 27 grams protein per serving.

BISCUIT DOUGH

Measure 2 cups all-purpose flour,* 3 teaspoons baking powder and 1 teaspoon salt into bowl. Cut in ¼ cup shortening thoroughly. Stir in *less than* ¾ cup milk. If dough is not pliable, add just enough additional milk to make a soft, puffy, easy-to-roll dough. Round up on floured cloth-covered board. Knead lightly 20 to 25 times, about ½ minute.

* If using self-rising flour, omit baking powder and salt.

TUNA PUFF CASSEROLE

1 can (6½ ounces) tuna, drained
1 can (10¾ ounces) condensed cream of mushroom soup
1 cup soft bread cubes
½ cup diced celery
¼ cup chopped pitted ripe olives
1 tablespoon finely chopped onion
½ teaspoon lemon juice
¼ cup mayonnaise or salad dressing
4 eggs, separated
¼ teaspoon red pepper sauce
⅓ cup milk

Heat oven to 325°. Mix tuna and half of the soup; stir in bread cubes, celery, olives, onion, lemon juice, mayonnaise and egg yolks.

Beat egg whites and pepper sauce until stiff but not dry; fold into tuna mixture. Pour into ungreased 1½-quart casserole. Bake until knife inserted in center comes out clean, 35 to 40 minutes.

Heat milk and remaining soup just to boiling, stirring frequently. Serve as a sauce with the casserole.

5 servings/about 18 grams protein per serving.

TUNA AND CHIPS

1 can (10¾ ounces) condensed cream of
   mushroom soup
½ cup milk
1 can (6½ ounces) tuna, drained
1¼ cups crushed potato chips
1 cup cooked green peas

Heat oven to 350°. Empty soup into ungreased 1-quart casserole; stir in milk. Stir
in tuna, 1 cup of the potato chips and the
peas. Sprinkle remaining potato chips over
top. Bake uncovered until heated through,
about 25 minutes.

4 servings/about 19 grams protein per
serving.

TUNA-SPINACH BAKE

2 packages (10 ounces each) frozen
   chopped spinach
¼ cup butter or margarine
¼ cup all-purpose flour
1 teaspoon salt
¼ teaspoon pepper
¼ teaspoon dry mustard
⅛ teaspoon onion salt
2 cups milk
½ cup mayonnaise or salad dressing
1 tablespoon lemon juice
1 can (6½ ounces) tuna, drained
1 cup croutons

Heat oven to 350°. Cook spinach as directed on package; drain.

Melt butter in saucepan over low heat.
Blend in flour and seasonings. Cook over
low heat, stirring constantly, until mixture
is smooth and bubbly. Remove from heat;
stir in milk. Heat to boiling, stirring constantly. Boil and stir 1 minute. Blend in
mayonnaise and lemon juice.

Spread tuna in ungreased baking dish,
10 × 6 × 1½ inches. Pour half of the sauce
over tuna. Mix remaining sauce and the
spinach; pour over tuna. Sprinkle with
croutons. Bake uncovered until bubbly, 25
to 30 minutes.

5 servings/about 17 grams protein per
serving.

TUNA ORIENTAL

1 tablespoon butter or margarine
1 cup cut-up celery
¼ cup chopped onion
2 tablespoons chopped green pepper
½ can (5½-ounce size) chow mein
   noodles
1 can (6½ ounces) tuna, drained
1 can (10¾ ounces) condensed cream of
   mushroom soup
¼ cup milk
¼ cup water
⅛ teaspoon pepper
¾ cup cashew nuts

Heat oven to 350°. Melt butter in large
skillet. Add celery, onion and green pepper;
cook and stir until onion is tender. Reserve
¼ cup chow mein noodles; stir in remaining ingredients.

Pour mixture into ungreased 1½-quart casserole; sprinkle reserved chow mein noodles
over top. Bake uncovered until mixture is
bubbly, about 30 minutes.

4 servings/about 19 grams protein per
serving.

CHOW MEIN LOAF

⅓ cup butter or margarine
⅓ cup all-purpose flour
¾ teaspoon salt
¼ teaspoon pepper
3 cups milk
2 eggs, separated
1 can (6½ ounces) tuna, drained
½ cup toasted slivered almonds
2 cups chow mein noodles
2 tablespoons capers

Heat oven to 350°. Melt butter over low heat in saucepan. Blend in flour and seasonings. Cook over low heat, stirring constantly, until mixture is smooth and bubbly. Remove from heat; stir in milk. Heat to boiling, stirring constantly. Boil and stir 1 minute.

Beat egg yolks slightly. Mix egg yolks, tuna, almonds, noodles and 1¼ cups of the sauce. Beat egg whites until stiff but not dry. Fold egg whites into tuna mixture.

Pour into well-greased loaf pan, 9 × 5 × 3 inches. Bake uncovered 30 minutes. Stir capers into remaining sauce; heat through. Unmold loaf on hot platter; serve with sauce.

5 servings/about 16 grams protein per serving.

SOUP AND CRACKER CASSEROLE

1 can (10½ ounces) condensed chicken with rice soup
1 can (10¾ ounces) condensed cream of mushroom soup
2 cans (6½ ounces each) tuna, drained
1 can (3 ounces) sliced mushrooms, drained
1 jar (2 ounces) pimiento, cut up
½ cup chopped green pepper
1 small onion, chopped
¼ teaspoon pepper
¼ cup toasted chopped almonds
3 cups oyster crackers
6 tomato slices
Parsley

Heat oven to 350°. Mix soups thoroughly; stir in remaining ingredients except tomato slices and parsley. Pour into greased baking dish, 11¾ × 7½ × 1¾ inches. Bake uncovered 30 to 35 minutes. Garnish with tomato slices and parsley.

6 servings/about 23 grams protein per serving.

HOW DO YOU LIKE YOUR CANNED TUNA?

Solid pack, chunk-style, grated or flaked? The practical approach is to use the costlier solid pack where appearance counts, the medium-priced chunk-style in casseroles and the less expensive grated or flaked tuna for sandwiches and dips. Whatever your preference, tuna is always a very good protein bargain. And this book offers over 25 different ways to try it.

TUNA PIZZA

¾ cup chopped onion
2 cans (8 ounces each) tomato sauce
1 can (6½ ounces) tuna, drained
1 can (8 ounces) sliced mushrooms, drained
½ teaspoon salt
¼ teaspoon pepper
1 package active dry yeast
⅔ cup warm water (105 to 115°)
2½ cups biscuit baking mix
2½ cups shredded mozzarella cheese
3 to 4 teaspoons oregano leaves

Heat oven to 425°. Mix onion, tomato sauce, tuna, mushrooms, salt and pepper; set aside.

Dissolve yeast in warm water. Stir in baking mix; beat vigorously. Turn dough onto surface well dusted with flour. Knead until smooth, about 20 times. Allow dough to rest a few minutes.

Divide dough into 4 pieces. Roll each piece very thin into a circle about 10 inches in diameter. Place on ungreased baking sheets or in shallow pie pans. Pinch edge of dough to make a slight rim. Spread tuna mixture over circles. Sprinkle shredded cheese over top. Sprinkle with oregano. Bake until crust is brown and filling hot and bubbly, 15 to 20 minutes. Cut into wedges; serve immediately.

Four 10-inch pizzas/about 30 grams protein per pizza.

VARIATION

Anchovy Pizza: Substitute 2 cans (2 ounces each) anchovies, drained and chopped, for the tuna.

About 28 grams protein per serving.

TUNA-VEGETABLE CHOWDER

1 cup diced uncooked potato (1 medium)
1 cup cut-up fresh or canned tomatoes
2 medium onions, cut into ¼-inch slices
¾ teaspoon celery seed
2 cups water
3 tablespoons butter or margarine
3 tablespoons flour
1¼ teaspoons salt
¼ teaspoon pepper
3 cups milk
2 cans (6½ ounces each) tuna, drained
Snipped chives or parsley

Heat potato, tomatoes, onions, celery seed and water to boiling in saucepan. Cover and cook over medium heat until potato is tender, about 15 minutes.

Melt butter over low heat. Blend in flour and seasonings. Cook over low heat, stirring constantly, until mixture is smooth and bubbly. Remove from heat; stir in milk. Heat to boiling, stirring constantly. Boil and stir 1 minute. Add tuna to potato mixture; stir in sauce. Sprinkle with chives.

6 servings, 1½ cups each/about 24 grams protein per serving.

CREAMY TUNA-CHEESE MOLD

1 envelope unflavored gelatin
⅓ cup cold water
½ cup boiling water
¾ cup diced celery
¼ cup finely chopped onion
¼ cup chopped green pepper
1 can (9¼ ounces) tuna, drained
½ teaspoon salt
½ teaspoon lemon pepper
½ cup shredded sharp Cheddar cheese
⅓ cup mayonnaise or salad dressing

Sprinkle gelatin on cold water to soften. Stir boiling water gradually into gelatin; stir until gelatin is dissolved. Mix in remaining ingredients. Pour salad into 4-cup mold. Cover and refrigerate until firm.

Just before serving, loosen salad from mold; invert on serving plate. Garnish with greens if desired.

5 servings/about 18 grams protein per serving.

TUNA SALAD IN CARAWAY PUFF BOWL

½ cup water
¼ cup butter or margarine
½ cup all-purpose flour
⅛ teaspoon salt
½ to 1 teaspoon caraway seed
2 eggs
Tuna Salad (right)

Heat oven to 400°. Grease 9-inch glass pie pan. Heat water and butter to a rolling boil. Quickly stir in flour, salt and caraway seed. Stir vigorously over low heat until mixture forms a ball, about 1 minute. Remove from heat. Beat in eggs, both at one time; continue beating until smooth. Spread batter evenly in pie pan (have batter touching side of pie pan, but do not spread up side). Bake 45 to 50 minutes.

Just before serving, mound Tuna Salad in caraway puff bowl. If desired, garnish with parsley, sliced tomatoes or hard-cooked eggs. Cut into wedges.

8 servings/about 19 grams protein per serving.

TUNA SALAD

2 cans (6½ ounces each) tuna, drained
1 cup cut-up celery
½ cup cubed avocado or ½ cup chopped
    green or ripe olives
¼ cup chopped onion
1 tablespoon lemon juice
3 hard-cooked eggs, cut up
½ teaspoon curry powder (optional)
¾ to 1 cup mayonnaise or salad dressing

Mix all ingredients except mayonnaise. Cover and refrigerate. Just before serving, fold mayonnaise into tuna mixture.

VARIATION

Chicken Salad in Caraway Puff Bowl: Substitute 2 cups cut-up cooked chicken for the tuna.

About 16 grams protein per serving.

TUNA-CHEESE SALAD

1 package (6 or 7 ounces) shell macaroni
1 cup cubed Cheddar cheese
1 can (6½ ounces) tuna, drained
¾ cup sliced sweet pickles
⅓ cup finely chopped onion
1 cup mayonnaise or salad dressing
¾ teaspoon salt
¼ teaspoon pepper
2 cloves garlic, crushed

Cook macaroni as directed on package; drain and rinse in cold water.

Combine macaroni, cheese, tuna, pickles and onion. Mix mayonnaise, salt, pepper and garlic. Pour over macaroni mixture; toss. Cover; refrigerate at least 3 hours.

6 servings/about 17 grams protein per serving.

TUNA ON A SHOESTRING

1 can (6½ ounces) tuna, drained
1 cup shredded carrots
1 cup diced celery
¼ cup finely chopped onion
¾ to 1 cup mayonnaise or salad dressing
1 can (4 ounces) shoestring potatoes
⅓ cup cashew nuts

Mix tuna, carrots, celery, onion and mayonnaise. Cover and refrigerate.

Just before serving, fold in potatoes and nuts. If desired, garnish with parsley and carrot curls.

4 servings/about 16 grams protein per serving.

HOT TUNA SUPPER SALAD

2 cans (6½ ounces each) tuna, drained
2 cups thinly sliced celery
1 cup toasted bread cubes
1 cup mayonnaise or salad dressing
½ cup toasted slivered almonds
2 tablespoons lemon juice
¼ cup chopped onion
½ teaspoon salt
½ cup shredded Cheddar cheese
1 cup toasted bread cubes or crushed
   potato chips

Heat oven to 350°. Mix all ingredients except cheese and 1 cup bread cubes. Pile into 6 ungreased individual casseroles or ungreased 2-quart casserole. Sprinkle with cheese and 1 cup bread cubes.

Bake until bubbly, 20 to 25 minutes for individual casseroles, 30 to 35 minutes for 2-quart casserole.

6 servings/about 23 grams protein per serving.

VARIATION

Hot Chicken Supper Salad: Substitute 2 cups cut-up cooked chicken or turkey for the tuna.

About 21 grams protein per serving.

BARBECUED TUNA SANDWICHES

½ cup catsup
1 package (3 ounces) cream cheese, softened
1 can (6½ ounces) tuna, drained
2 tablespoons finely chopped celery
2 tablespoons finely chopped green pepper
1 tablespoon pickle relish or 2 teaspoons wine vinegar
1 teaspoon finely chopped onion
½ teaspoon horseradish
½ teaspoon Worcestershire sauce
3 hamburger buns, split
Soft butter or margarine
¾ cup shredded American cheese

Blend catsup and cream cheese; mix in tuna, celery, green pepper, pickle relish, onion, horseradish and Worcestershire sauce.

Spread buns with butter; place on baking sheet. Spoon tuna mixture on each bun half; sprinkle with cheese.

Set oven control at broil and/or 550°. Place baking sheet under broiler with tops of sandwiches 5 inches from heat; broil until cheese melts.

6 sandwiches/about 16 grams protein per sandwich.

VARIATION

Barbecued Chicken Sandwiches: Substitute 2 cans (5½ ounces each) boned chicken or 1½ cups cut-up cooked chicken or turkey for the tuna.

About 16 grams protein per sandwich.

TUNA CHEESIES

1 can (6½ ounces) tuna, drained
¼ cup finely chopped onion
¼ cup chopped celery
2 tablespoons mayonnaise or salad dressing
¼ teaspoon salt
¼ teaspoon pepper
8 slices toast
Soft butter or margarine
8 slices tomato
8 slices process American cheese
Mayonnaise or salad dressing

Mix tuna, onion, celery, 2 tablespoons mayonnaise, the salt and pepper. Spread toast with butter; place on baking sheet.

Spread tuna mixture on each toast slice; top with tomato slice. Trim cheese to fit bread; place on top of tomato. Spread cheese with mayonnaise.

Set oven control at broil and/or 550°. Place baking sheet under broiler with tops of sandwiches 5 inches from heat; broil until cheese is melted, 3 to 5 minutes.

8 sandwiches/about 16 grams protein per serving.

Note: 4 English muffins, halved, or 8 rusks can be substituted for the toast.

SALMON 'N PASTA

1⅓ cups uncooked elbow macaroni
    (5 ounces)
1 can (16 ounces) salmon, drained
    (reserve liquid)
¼ cup butter or margarine
½ cup chopped onion
2 tablespoons flour
1¾ cups milk
½ teaspoon salt
⅛ teaspoon paprika
1 tablespoon lemon juice
¼ cup snipped parsley
2 cups shredded Cheddar cheese (about
    8 ounces)

Heat oven to 375°. Cook macaroni as directed on package; drain.

Flake salmon, removing bone and skin. Melt butter in saucepan. Add onion; cook and stir until tender. Blend in flour. Cook over low heat, stirring constantly, until mixture is bubbly. Remove from heat; stir in reserved salmon liquid and the milk. Heat to boiling, stirring constantly. Boil and stir 1 minute. Remove from heat; stir in salt, paprika, lemon juice and parsley.

Layer macaroni, salmon and ¾ of the cheese in ungreased 2-quart casserole. Pour sauce over; sprinkle with remaining cheese. Bake uncovered until sauce is bubbly, 20 to 25 minutes.

8 servings/about 21 grams protein per serving.

VARIATION

Tuna 'n Pasta: Substitute 2 cans (6½ ounces each) tuna, well drained, for the salmon; increase milk to 2 cups.

About 18 grams protein per serving.

SCALLOPED SALMON

4 ounces uncooked egg noodles
1 tablespoon butter or margarine
1 tablespoon flour
1 teaspoon salt
¼ teaspoon pepper
1 cup milk
1 can (7¾ ounces) salmon, drained
1 to 2 tablespoons lemon juice
½ cup toasted sliced or slivered almonds

Heat oven to 350°. Cook noodles as directed on package; drain.

Melt butter in saucepan. Blend in flour and seasonings. Cook over low heat, stirring constantly, until mixture is smooth and bubbly. Remove from heat; stir in milk. Heat to boiling, stirring constantly. Boil and stir 1 minute. Remove from heat.

Flake salmon, removing bone and skin. Sprinkle lemon juice over salmon. Add noodles, almonds and sauce; toss lightly. Turn into 5 ungreased individual shells or baking dishes or a 1-quart casserole. Bake until bubbly, 10 to 15 minutes for shells and dishes, 20 minutes for casserole.

5 servings/about 16 grams protein per serving.

SALMON ROMANOFF

8 ounces uncooked egg noodles
1 can (16 ounces) salmon, drained
1½ cups creamed cottage cheese
1 cup dairy sour cream
½ cup finely chopped onion
1 clove garlic, finely chopped
1 to 2 teaspoons Worcestershire sauce
Dash of red pepper sauce
½ teaspoon salt
½ cup shredded sharp cheese

Heat oven to 325°. Cook noodles as directed on package; drain.

Flake salmon, removing bone and skin. Mix salmon, noodles, cottage cheese, sour cream, onion, garlic, Worcestershire sauce, red pepper sauce and salt. Pour into greased 2-quart casserole. Sprinkle with cheese. Bake uncovered until bubbly, about 40 minutes. If desired, garnish with parsley and lemon slices.

8 servings/about 22 grams protein per serving.

Note: Salmon Romanoff is pictured on the back cover—top row, at right.

VARIATION

Tuna Romanoff: Substitute 2 cans (6½ ounces each) tuna, drained, for the salmon.

About 25 grams protein per serving.

STUFFED SALMON LOAF

1 can (16 ounces) salmon, drained
1 egg, slightly beaten
2 tablespoons milk
½ teaspoon salt
⅛ teaspoon pepper
Stuffing (below)
3 tablespoons snipped parsley

Heat oven to 350°. Flake salmon, removing bone and skin. Mix salmon, egg, milk, salt and pepper. Press in bottom and against sides of greased loaf pan, 9 x 5 x 3 inches.

Spoon half of the Stuffing over salmon mixture; press firmly. Sprinkle parsley over Stuffing. Cover with remaining Stuffing; press firmly. Bake uncovered 50 minutes. If desired, serve with a cheese sauce.

6 servings/about 17 grams protein per serving.

STUFFING

3 tablespoons butter or margarine
½ cup chopped celery
1 tablespoon chopped onion
¼ cup milk
½ teaspoon salt
¼ teaspoon pepper
½ to 1 teaspoon sage
1½ cups soft bread crumbs

Melt butter in saucepan. Add celery and onion; cook and stir until tender. Remove from heat; stir in milk, salt, pepper, sage and bread crumbs.

SALMON TURNOVERS

1 package (11 or 22 ounces) pie crust
   sticks or mix
1 can (7¾ ounces) salmon, drained
1 tablespoon mayonnaise or salad dressing
1 teaspoon lemon juice
Cucumber Sauce (below)

Heat oven to 425°. Prepare pastry for Two-crust Pie as directed on package except—roll pastry into rectangle, 16 × 12 inches. Cut rectangle into twelve 4-inch squares with pastry wheel or knife.

Flake salmon, removing bone and skin. Stir mayonnaise and lemon juice into salmon. Place about 1 tablespoon salmon filling on each square of pastry. Moisten edges of each square with water. Fold pastry over to make triangles; press edges together to seal. Prick tops with fork. Bake on ungreased baking sheet until golden brown, 15 to 20 minutes. Serve hot with Cucumber Sauce.

4 servings/about 23 grams protein per serving.

CUCUMBER SAUCE
¼ cup butter or margarine
¼ cup all-purpose flour
½ teaspoon salt
⅛ teaspoon pepper
2 cups milk
1 cup diced pared cucumber

Melt butter over low heat in saucepan. Blend in flour and seasonings. Cook over low heat, stirring constantly, until mixture is smooth and bubbly. Remove from heat; stir in milk. Heat to boiling, stirring constantly. Boil and stir 1 minute. Stir in cucumber; simmer 10 minutes.

SALMON-MACARONI SLAW

¾ cup uncooked elbow macaroni
   (3 ounces)
1 can (16 ounces) salmon, drained
3 cups finely shredded cabbage
½ cup chopped celery
1 green pepper, chopped
2 tablespoons finely chopped onion
1½ teaspoons salt
½ teaspoon pepper
¼ cup salad oil
2 tablespoons vinegar

Cook macaroni as directed on package; drain and rinse in cold water. Flake salmon, removing bone and skin.

Mix macaroni, salmon, cabbage, celery, green pepper and onion. Mix salt, pepper, oil and vinegar; pour over macaroni mixture and toss. Refrigerate ½ hour. If a moister salad is desired, stir in ⅔ cup mayonnaise or salad dressing.

6 servings/about 17 grams protein per serving.

VARIATIONS
Shrimp-Macaroni Slaw: Substitute 3 cans (4½ ounces each) shrimp, rinsed and drained, for the salmon.

About 16 grams protein per serving.

Tuna-Macaroni Slaw: Substitute 1 can (9¼ ounces) tuna, drained, for the salmon. Stir in ½ cup shredded Cheddar cheese.

About 16 grams protein per serving.

CREOLE FLOUNDER

2 pounds flounder or haddock fillets
1½ cups chopped tomatoes
½ cup chopped green pepper
⅓ cup lemon juice
1 tablespoon salad oil
2 teaspoons salt
2 teaspoons instant minced onion
1 teaspoon basil leaves
¼ teaspoon coarsely ground pepper
4 drops red pepper sauce

Heat oven to 500°. Place fish in greased baking dish, 13½ × 9 × 2 inches. Mix remaining ingredients; spoon over fish. Bake uncovered until fish flakes easily with fork, 5 to 8 minutes.

8 servings/about 19 grams protein per serving.

Note: Creole Flounder is pictured on the front cover—bottom row, at left.

HADDOCK IN CHEESE SAUCE

2 tablespoons butter or margarine
1 tablespoon finely chopped onion
2 tablespoons flour
1 teaspoon salt
¼ teaspoon pepper
1 cup milk
1 cup shredded process American cheese
    (about 4 ounces)
Salt
1½ pounds haddock fillets
Juice of ½ lemon
1 tablespoon snipped parsley

Heat oven to 350°. Melt butter over low heat in saucepan. Add onion; cook and stir until tender. Blend in flour, 1 teaspoon salt and the pepper. Cook over low heat, stirring constantly, until mixture is bubbly. Remove from heat; stir in milk. Heat to boiling, stirring constantly. Boil and stir 1 minute. Remove from heat; stir in cheese until melted.

Sprinkle salt over fish. Place in lightly greased shallow pan. Squeeze lemon juice over fish; pour sauce over. Bake uncovered 25 minutes. Sprinkle with parsley.

8 servings/about 20 grams protein per serving.

BAKED FISH WITH MUSHROOM SAUCE

2 packages (1 pound each) frozen fish
    fillets (sole, cod, halibut or haddock)
½ teaspoon thyme (optional)
1 can (10¾ ounces) condensed cream of
    mushroom soup
2 small tomatoes
1 to 2 tablespoons soft butter or margarine
Parsley flakes or dill weed

Thaw fillets just until they can be separated.

Heat oven to 475°. Arrange fillets in ungreased baking dish, 13½ × 9 × 2 inches. Stir thyme into mushroom soup; spread over fish.

Bake uncovered 30 minutes. Slice tomatoes; cut each slice in half and place on fish. Brush butter over tomatoes; sprinkle with parsley. Bake uncovered until fish flakes easily with fork, about 5 minutes longer.

8 servings/about 22 grams protein per serving.

HALIBUT LOAF WITH ALMOND SAUCE

4 cups soft bread crumbs
1 cup light cream
1 pound halibut, cut into small pieces
1 teaspoon salt
¼ teaspoon celery salt
1 teaspoon butter or margarine, melted
4 egg whites
Almond Sauce (below)

Heat oven to 350°. Mix crumbs, cream, halibut, salt, celery salt and butter. Beat egg whites until stiff but not dry. Fold egg whites into halibut mixture. Pour into well-greased loaf pan, 9 × 5 × 3 inches. Place in pan of hot water. Bake uncovered 40 to 50 minutes. Serve with Almond Sauce.

8 servings/about 20 grams protein per serving.

ALMOND SAUCE

3 tablespoons butter or margarine
4 ounces slivered blanched almonds
2 tablespoons flour
½ teaspoon salt
2 cups light cream

Melt butter in saucepan. Add almonds; cook and stir until brown. Blend in flour and salt. Cook over low heat, stirring constantly, until mixture is bubbly. Remove from heat; stir in cream. Heat to boiling, stirring constantly. Boil and stir 1 minute.

SIMPLE SAUCY FISH BAKE

1 package (1 pound) fresh or frozen
    ocean perch fillets
½ teaspoon salt
⅛ teaspoon pepper
1 tablespoon butter or margarine
1 package (1¾ ounces) Hollandaise sauce
    mix
1 can (19 ounces) asparagus spears,
    drained, or 1 package (10 ounces)
    frozen asparagus spears, cooked and
    drained
Paprika
1 can (3½ ounces) French fried onions

If frozen, thaw fillets just until they can be separated. Skin fillets, if desired.

Heat oven to 475°. Sprinkle both sides of fillets with salt. Arrange fillets in ungreased baking dish, 11¾ × 7½ × 1¾ inches, leaving a space in center of dish. Sprinkle with pepper and dot with butter. Bake uncovered 15 minutes.

Prepare Hollandaise sauce mix as directed on package. Remove fish from oven. Place asparagus spears in center of dish. Pour hot Hollandaise sauce over asparagus. Sprinkle sauce with paprika.

Bake uncovered until fish is done, about 5 minutes. Sprinkle onions over fish. Bake until onions are golden brown, about 2 minutes.

5 servings/about 20 grams protein per serving.

FISH CASSEROLE ENCORE

3 tablespoons butter or margarine
3 tablespoons flour
½ teaspoon salt
¼ teaspoon onion salt
¼ teaspoon pepper
⅛ teaspoon mace
1½ cups milk
1 egg yolk, slightly beaten
1 tablespoon snipped parsley
1 tablespoon lemon juice
1 pound flaked cooked fish (2 cups)
¼ cup buttered cracker crumbs

Heat oven to 400°. Melt butter over low heat in saucepan. Blend in flour and seasonings. Cook over low heat, stirring constantly, until mixture is smooth and bubbly. Remove from heat; stir in milk. Heat to boiling, stirring constantly. Boil and stir 1 minute.

Pour at least half of the hot mixture into egg yolk; blend into remaining mixture in saucepan. Boil 1 minute. Remove from heat; stir in parsley and lemon juice.

Alternate layers of sauce and fish in greased 1-quart casserole. Top with cracker crumbs. Bake uncovered until brown, about 25 minutes.

6 servings/about 17 grams protein per serving.

HAWAIIAN HALIBUT

2 halibut steaks (1 pound each)
3 teaspoons salt
2 teaspoons butter or margarine
1 cup boiling water
1 cup uncooked instant rice
2 cups soft bread cubes
2 tablespoons lemon juice
1 can (20 ounces) crushed pineapple, drained
1 teaspoon curry powder

Heat oven to 350°. Sprinkle steaks with 1 teaspoon of the salt. Place in ungreased baking dish, 11¾ × 7½ × 1¾ inches. Stir 1 teaspoon salt and the butter into boiling water; add rice. Cover; let stand 5 minutes.

Mix rice, bread cubes, lemon juice, pineapple, curry powder and 1 teaspoon salt; sprinkle over fish. Cover with aluminum foil. Bake 20 minutes. Remove foil and bake 20 minutes longer.

8 servings/about 25 grams protein per serving.

BUYING FRESH FISH

Don't be squeamish, now. Eyes should be clear and bulging, gills reddish-pink, scales bright, flesh firm and no "fishy" odor. And what's a fillet? Fish sides, cut lengthwise away from the backbone. Practically boneless, with little or no waste. Allow ⅓ to ½ pound per serving. Store in coldest section of refrigerator right away!

CURRIED HADDOCK IN POLKA-DOT RING

1 pound haddock fillets
½ cup water
¼ teaspoon salt
2 tablespoons butter or margarine
¼ cup finely chopped onion
2 tablespoons flour
1 teaspoon curry powder
1 teaspoon sugar
¼ teaspoon salt
Dash of ginger
¾ cup milk
3 cups hot cooked rice
1 package (10 ounces) frozen peas,
    cooked and drained
1 tablespoon chopped pimiento
Lemon wedges

Heat haddock, water and ¼ teaspoon salt to boiling. Reduce heat; cover and simmer until fish flakes easily with fork, 6 to 10 minutes. Drain; reserve ½ cup broth. Break fillets into 2-inch pieces; keep warm while preparing sauce.

Melt butter in saucepan. Add onion; cook and stir until tender. Stir in flour, curry powder, sugar, ¼ teaspoon salt and the ginger. Cook over low heat, stirring constantly, until mixture is bubbly. Remove from heat; stir in reserved broth and the milk. Heat to boiling, stirring constantly. Boil and stir 1 minute. Stir in fish; heat through.

Mix rice and peas. Lightly press in well-buttered 6½-cup ring mold. Invert ring on platter. Fill center with fish mixture. Garnish with pimiento and lemon wedges.

6 servings/about 19 grams protein per serving.

FISH CHOWDER

1 pound haddock or cod
1 cup water
1 tablespoon butter or margarine
1 medium onion, sliced
1 large potato, pared and diced
½ cup chopped celery
½ bay leaf, crumbled
1 teaspoon salt
¼ teaspoon pepper
2 cups milk
1 tablespoon butter or margarine
4 teaspoons bacon-flavored vegetable
    protein chips

Heat haddock and water to boiling. Reduce heat; cover and simmer 15 minutes.

Remove fish from broth. Measure broth; add water to measure 1½ cups. Remove bones from fish.

Melt 1 tablespoon butter in large saucepan. Add onion slices; cook and stir until tender. Stir in fish, potato, celery, bay leaf, salt, pepper and broth. Heat to boiling. Reduce heat; cover and simmer 30 minutes. Stir in milk and 1 tablespoon butter; simmer 5 minutes longer. Pour into serving bowls; sprinkle each serving with 1 teaspoon protein chips.

4 servings, 2 cups each/about 25 grams protein per serving.

SKILLET PAELLA

1 package (12 ounces) frozen peeled
  shrimp
1 can (7 to 8 ounces) minced clams
1 can (5 ounces) boned chicken
1 can (16 ounces) tomatoes
1 package (10 ounces) frozen green peas,
  broken apart
2 cups uncooked instant rice
2 tablespoons instant minced onion
  or ⅓ cup finely chopped onion
1 teaspoon paprika
1 teaspoon instant chicken bouillon or 1
  chicken bouillon cube
¼ teaspoon cayenne red pepper
⅛ teaspoon saffron

Rinse frozen shrimp under cold running
water to remove ice crystals. Stir together
clams (with liquor) and remaining ingredients in large skillet.

Heat to boiling, stirring occasionally. Reduce
heat; simmer 5 minutes. Remove from heat.
Cover tightly; let stand about 10 minutes.

6 servings/about 26 grams protein per
serving.

Substitutions
For frozen shrimp: 2 cans (4½ ounces
each) jumbo shrimp, drained.
For canned chicken: ½ cup cut-up cooked
chicken.
For tomatoes: 1 can (16 ounces) stewed
tomatoes.

SHRIMP AND MUSHROOMS

2 cups sliced celery
2 cans (3 ounces each) sliced
  mushrooms, drained (reserve liquid)
1 tablespoon soy sauce
1 teaspoon ginger
2 tablespoons cornstarch
2 tablespoons cold water
1 teaspoon instant beef bouillon
1 cup water
2 cans (4½ ounces each) shrimp, rinsed
  and drained
2 cups hot cooked rice

Cook and stir celery, reserved mushroom
liquid, soy sauce and ginger in large skillet
until celery is crisp-tender, about 5 minutes.

Mix cornstarch and 2 tablespoons water
until smooth. Stir cornstarch mixture,
bouillon and 1 cup water into celery. Cook,
stirring constantly, until mixture thickens
and boils. Boil and stir 1 minute. Stir in
shrimp and mushrooms; heat through,
stirring frequently. Serve over rice.

4 servings/about 18 grams protein per
serving.

THE BEAUTY OF SHRIMP

*It's here all year around, canned or frozen
and in various sizes. Canned is easy to
keep on the shelf and chill at the last
moment. But frozen is the next best thing
to fresh; and frozen individually, you can
shake out a few and return the rest to the
freezer. Both kinds take well to stretching
with rice, pasta and sauces.*

SHRIMP AND POTATO SOUFFLE

Instant mashed potato puffs (enough for
  4 servings)
3 eggs, separated
1 tablespoon snipped chives
1 tablespoon finely chopped onion
1 can (4½ ounces) shrimp, rinsed and
  drained

Heat oven to 350°. Prepare potato puffs as
directed on package. Beat egg whites until
soft peaks form. Beat egg yolks slightly;
stir egg yolks, chives, onion and shrimp into
potatoes. Carefully fold in egg whites.

Turn into greased 1½-quart casserole; place
in pan of hot water (1 inch deep). Bake
until golden brown and nicely puffed, 50 to
60 minutes. If desired, serve with a cheese
sauce.

4 servings/about 16 grams protein per
serving.

SEAFOOD A LA NEWBURG

¼ cup butter or margarine
¼ cup all-purpose flour
½ teaspoon salt
¼ teaspoon pepper
2 cups milk
2 egg yolks, beaten
1 tablespoon lemon juice
2 cups cooked seafood (large pieces)
8 slices toast

Melt butter over low heat in saucepan.
Blend in flour and seasonings. Cook over
low heat, stirring constantly, until mixture

is smooth and bubbly. Remove from heat;
stir in milk. Heat to boiling, stirring constantly. Boil and stir 1 minute.

Pour at least half of the hot mixture into
egg yolks; blend into remaining mixture
in saucepan. Stir in lemon juice and seafood; heat through. Serve hot over toast.

8 servings/about 19 grams protein per
serving.

SEAFOOD AND RICE

¼ cup butter or margarine
3 cups cooked seafood (large pieces)
2 tablespoons lemon juice
1 can (10¾ ounces) condensed cream of
  shrimp soup
1 cup milk
3 cups hot cooked rice
¼ cup buttered bread crumbs

Melt butter in saucepan. Add seafood; cook
and stir until heated through. Stir in lemon
juice, soup and milk; heat through, stirring
frequently. Serve over rice; sprinkle with
bread crumbs.

6 servings/about 16 grams protein per
serving.

OYSTERS CREMEUX

6 ounces uncooked egg noodles
Milk
2 cans (8 ounces each) oysters, drained
    (reserve liquor)
½ cup butter or margarine,
    softened
1 egg
1 tablespoon flour
1 clove garlic, crushed
½ teaspoon bottled brown bouquet sauce
¼ teaspoon mace
Dash of cayenne red pepper
2 cups shredded process sharp American
    cheese (about 8 ounces)
3 tablespoons snipped parsley
¼ teaspoon freshly ground pepper
¼ cup buttered bread crumbs

Heat oven to 350°. Cook noodles as directed on package; drain.

Add milk to reserved oyster liquor to measure 2 cups. Heat oysters and liquid in large skillet over medium-high heat about 5 minutes.

Blend butter, egg, flour, garlic, bouquet sauce, mace and cayenne pepper; stir slowly into skillet. Heat to boiling over medium heat, stirring constantly. Boil and stir 1 minute. Mix in noodles, 1¾ cups of the cheese, the parsley and pepper.

Pour into ungreased 2-quart casserole. Sprinkle with remaining cheese and the bread crumbs. Bake uncovered until bubbly, about 20 minutes.

6 servings/about 24 grams protein per serving.

CLAM SQUARES WITH SHRIMP SAUCE

3 cups cooked rice
¼ cup chopped onion
¼ cup snipped parsley
1 jar (2 ounces) chopped pimiento,
    drained
1 cup shredded sharp Cheddar cheese
    (about 4 ounces)
1 teaspoon salt
1 teaspoon Worcestershire sauce
1 can (7 to 8 ounces) minced clams,
    drained
3 eggs, slightly beaten
2 cups milk
Shrimp Sauce (below)

Heat oven to 325°. Combine all ingredients except Shrimp Sauce. Pour into ungreased baking dish, 13½ × 9 × 2 inches. Bake uncovered 45 minutes. Cut into squares; serve Shrimp Sauce over squares.

6 servings/about 20 grams protein per serving.

SHRIMP SAUCE

1 can (10¾ ounces) condensed cream of
    shrimp soup
½ cup dairy sour cream
1 teaspoon lemon juice
¼ teaspoon salt

Heat all ingredients in small saucepan just to boiling, stirring frequently.

CLAM SOUFFLE

2 cans (7 to 8 ounces each) minced
  clams, drained (reserve 1 cup liquor)
2 cups soft bread crumbs
4 eggs, separated
1 tablespoon butter or margarine,
  melted
½ cup milk
¾ teaspoon salt
⅛ teaspoon pepper

Heat oven to 350°. Mix clams, reserved liquor and crumbs; let stand 10 minutes. Beat egg yolks, butter, milk, salt and pepper into clam mixture.

Beat egg whites until stiff but not dry; fold into clam mixture. Pour into greased loaf pan, 9 × 5 × 3 inches. Bake uncovered 40 minutes. Serve with a favorite sauce.

4 servings/about 16 grams protein per serving.

CLAM SPAGHETTI

7 or 8 ounces uncooked spaghetti
1 can (10 ounces) minced clams
¼ cup butter or margarine
2 cloves garlic, finely chopped
2 tablespoons snipped parsley
Snipped parsley
½ cup grated Parmesan cheese

Cook spaghetti as directed on package; drain.

Drain clams, reserving liquor. Melt butter in saucepan; add garlic. Cook and stir until light brown. Stir in clams, liquor and 2 tablespoons parsley. Heat to boiling. Reduce heat; simmer 3 to 5 minutes. Pour over hot spaghetti and mix gently. Sprinkle with parsley and cheese.

4 servings/about 23 grams protein per serving.

VARIATION

Oyster Spaghetti: Substitute 1 can (8 ounces) oysters, finely chopped, for the clams.

About 20 grams protein per serving.

EASY NEW ENGLAND CLAM CHOWDER

2 tablespoons butter or margarine
¼ cup finely chopped onion
1 can (10¾ ounces) condensed cream of
  potato soup
¾ cup milk
2 cans (7 to 8 ounces each) minced
  clams
1 tablespoon lemon juice
⅛ teaspoon pepper
4 teaspoons bacon-flavored vegetable
  protein chips

Melt butter in large saucepan. Add onion; cook and stir until tender. Stir in soup and milk; heat through. Stir in clams (with liquor), lemon juice and pepper. Heat through, stirring occasionally. Just before serving, sprinkle with protein chips.

3 servings, 1⅓ cups each/about 16 grams protein per serving.

cheese, eggs & beans

Let them eat cheese. Or eggs. Or beans. These foods are capable of many delicious meatless meals. Cheese melts readily into a Welsh Rarebit, exquisitely into Oven Cheese Fondue. Eggs go continental in French Omelet or Spinach Frittata. Or eggs combine with cheese for Eggs au Gratin en Casserole or fancier Egg Croquettes. And ever thought to experiment with a recipe like Crunchy Baked Soys? Or add coffee or brandy flavoring for Baked Bean Casserole? Great protein boosters. Great holdouts till payday. And certainly no apologies are needed for the most discriminating guests.

OVEN CHEESE FONDUE

10 slices white bread
6 eggs
3 cups milk
2 tablespoons snipped parsley
1 teaspoon dry mustard
1 teaspoon salt
2 cups shredded process sharp American cheese (about 8 ounces)
3 tablespoons finely chopped onion

Heat oven to 325°. Remove crusts from bread; cut bread into cubes. Beat eggs, milk and seasonings. Stir in bread cubes, cheese and onion. Pour into ungreased baking dish, 11¾ × 7½ × 1¾ inches.

Bake uncovered until knife inserted in center comes out clean, about 1 hour.

8 servings/about 17 grams protein per serving.

CONTINENTAL CHEESE BAKE

1 tablespoon butter or margarine
1 cup sliced onion
8 hard-cooked eggs, sliced
2 cups shredded process Swiss cheese
  (about 8 ounces)
1 can (10¾ ounces) condensed cream of
  mushroom soup
¾ cup milk
1 teaspoon prepared mustard
½ teaspoon seasoned salt
¼ teaspoon dill weed
¼ teaspoon pepper
6 slices caraway rye bread
Soft butter or margarine

Heat oven to 350°. Melt 1 tablespoon butter in small skillet. Add onion; cook and stir until tender. Spread in baking dish, 11¾ × 7½ × 1¾ inches. Top with egg slices; sprinkle with cheese.

Beat remaining ingredients except bread and soft butter with rotary beater. Pour soup mixture over cheese. Spread bread slices with butter; cut diagonally into 4 pieces. Overlap bread slices on top of casserole (buttered sides up).

Bake uncovered until heated through, 30 to 35 minutes. Set oven control at broil and/or 550°. Place casserole under broiler with top 5 inches from heat; broil until bread is toasted, about 1 minute.

6 servings/about 23 grams protein per serving.

CHEESE STRATA

10 slices white bread
⅓ cup soft butter or margarine
1 clove garlic, crushed
½ teaspoon dry mustard
2 cups shredded sharp Cheddar cheese
  (about 8 ounces)
2 tablespoons chopped onion
2 tablespoons snipped parsley
1 teaspoon salt
½ teaspoon Worcestershire sauce
⅛ teaspoon pepper
Dash of cayenne red pepper
4 eggs
2⅓ cups milk
⅔ cup dry white wine

Remove crusts from bread. Mix butter, garlic and mustard. Spread on bread slices; cut each slice into thirds. Line bottom and sides of ungreased baking dish, 8 × 8 × 2 inches, with some of the bread slices (buttered sides down).

Mix cheese, onion, parsley, salt, Worcestershire sauce, pepper and cayenne red pepper; spread evenly in baking dish. Top with remaining bread slices (buttered sides up). Beat eggs; blend in milk and wine. Pour over bread. Cover and refrigerate at least 2 hours.

Heat oven to 325°. Bake uncovered until knife inserted in center comes out clean, about 1¼ hours. Let stand 10 minutes before serving.

6 servings/about 21 grams protein per serving.

Note: If desired, omit wine and increase milk to 2½ cups.

CHEESE SOUFFLE DELUXE

¼ cup butter or margarine
¼ cup all-purpose flour
½ teaspoon salt
Dash of cayenne red pepper
1 cup milk
2 cups shredded Cheddar cheese (about 8 ounces)
6 eggs, separated

Heat oven to 300°. Melt butter in saucepan. Blend in flour and seasonings. Cook over low heat, stirring constantly, until mixture is smooth and bubbly. Remove from heat; stir in milk. Heat to boiling, stirring constantly. Boil and stir 1 minute. Remove from heat; stir in cheese until melted.

Beat egg whites until stiff but not dry; set aside. Beat egg yolks until very thick and lemon colored; stir into cheese mixture. Stir about ¼ of the egg whites into cheese mixture. Gently fold mixture into remaining egg whites. Pour into well-greased 2-quart casserole.

Bake until knife inserted in center comes out clean, about 1¼ hours.

4 servings/about 18 grams protein per serving.

Note: Cheese Soufflé Deluxe is pictured on the back cover—top row, center.

CHEDDAR-EGG BAKE

6 eggs, slightly beaten
1 cup shredded Cheddar cheese (about 4 ounces)
½ cup milk
2 tablespoons soft butter or margarine
1 teaspoon prepared mustard
½ teaspoon salt
¼ teaspoon pepper

Heat oven to 325°. Mix all ingredients. Pour into ungreased baking pan, 8 × 8 × 2 inches. Bake until knife inserted in center comes out clean, 25 to 30 minutes.

4 servings/about 18 grams protein per serving.

CHILI PEPPER CASSEROLE

3 eggs
1 cup milk
½ cup biscuit baking mix
½ teaspoon salt
2 cans (4 ounces each) roasted and peeled green chilies
2 cups chopped tomatoes (2 to 3 medium)
2 cups shredded Cheddar cheese (about 8 ounces)

Heat oven to 350°. Grease baking dish, 8 × 8 × 2 inches. Beat eggs, milk, baking mix and salt until foamy. Remove stems and seeds from chilies; rinse chilies with water. Spread in dish; sprinkle with tomatoes and cheese. Pour egg mixture over cheese mixture. Bake uncovered until golden, 40 to 45 minutes.

6 servings/about 16 grams protein per serving.

SPAGHETTI PIE

7 ounces uncooked spaghetti
1 cup creamed cottage cheese
2 eggs, slightly beaten
1½ teaspoons salt
⅛ teaspoon pepper
1 cup shredded sharp Cheddar cheese
  (about 4 ounces)
1 egg, beaten
2 tablespoons grated Parmesan cheese

Cook spaghetti as directed on package; drain.

Heat oven to 350°. Mix cottage cheese, 2 eggs, the salt, pepper, Cheddar cheese and spaghetti. Turn into buttered 9-inch pie pan. Mix 1 egg and the Parmesan cheese; spread over spaghetti mixture.

Bake until knife inserted in center comes out clean, 45 to 50 minutes. Cut into wedges; serve warm and, if desired, with Mushroom Sauce or Tomato Sauce (below).

5 servings/about 21 grams protein per serving.

MUSHROOM SAUCE
Heat 1 can (10¾ ounces) condensed cream of mushroom soup and ½ cup milk just to boiling, stirring frequently.

TOMATO SAUCE
1 tablespoon butter or margarine, melted
2 tablespoons chopped onion
2 tablespoons chopped green pepper
1 can (8 ounces) tomato sauce
Salt and pepper

Melt butter in small saucepan. Add onion and green pepper; cook and stir until tender. Stir in tomato sauce, salt and pepper; heat over low heat.

CONCORDIA SPAGHETTI

About 4 ounces uncooked spaghetti
¼ cup butter or margarine
¼ cup all-purpose flour
½ teaspoon salt
¼ teaspoon pepper
2 cups milk
½ cup shredded American cheese
¼ cup finely chopped green pepper
¼ cup finely chopped pimiento
3 hard-cooked eggs, chopped
¼ cup sliced pimiento-stuffed olives

Heat oven to 350°. Cook spaghetti as directed on package; drain.

Melt butter in saucepan over low heat. Blend in flour and seasonings. Cook over low heat, stirring constantly, until mixture is smooth and bubbly. Remove from heat; stir in milk. Heat to boiling, stirring constantly. Boil and stir 1 minute. Remove from heat; stir in cheese, pepper, pimiento and eggs until cheese is melted.

Mix cheese sauce and spaghetti. Pour into greased 1-quart casserole. Bake uncovered until golden brown, about 30 minutes. Garnish with olives.

4 servings/about 16 grams protein per serving.

TOSCANA PIE

1 tablespoon olive oil
3 tablespoons butter or margarine
½ cup chopped green onions (about 8)
Pinch of anise seed
16 ounces fresh spinach, finely chopped
3 chicken bouillon cubes
¼ teaspoon salt
¼ teaspoon pepper
2⅓ cups all-purpose flour*
½ teaspoon salt
1 cup shortening
½ to ⅔ cup cold water
1½ cups creamed cottage cheese
2 tablespoons grated Parmesan cheese
3 eggs, slightly beaten
2 tablespoons milk
1 teaspoon olive oil
1 egg

Heat 1 tablespoon olive oil and the butter in large saucepan. Add onions; cook and stir until tender. Stir in anise seed, spinach, bouillon cubes, ¼ teaspoon salt and the pepper. Cover; cook over low heat just until spinach is tender, 10 to 15 minutes. Remove from heat.

Heat oven to 350°. Measure flour and ½ teaspoon salt into bowl. Cut in shortening thoroughly. Sprinkle in water, 1 tablespoon at a time, mixing until flour is moistened and pastry almost cleans side of bowl. Gather into ball; shape into flattened circle. Roll pastry on floured cloth-covered board into rectangle, 20 × 15 inches. Cut crosswise in half; place one half in jelly roll pan, 15½ × 10½ × 1 inch.

Stir cheeses and 3 eggs into spinach mixture; spread over pastry in pan. Cut several slits in remaining pastry half; place over filling. Blend milk, 1 teaspoon olive oil and 1 egg; brush over top. Bake 1 hour.

6 servings/about 20 grams protein per serving.

* If using self-rising flour, omit ½ teaspoon salt. Pastry made with self-rising flour differs in flavor and texture.

CHEESE-VEGETABLE CASSEROLE

3 eggs
½ cup milk
½ cup biscuit baking mix
1 teaspoon salt
½ teaspoon cayenne red pepper
¼ teaspoon pepper
3 cups chopped zucchini
3 cups chopped tomatoes (3 to 4 medium)
2 cups shredded Cheddar cheese (about 8 ounces)

Heat oven to 350°. Grease baking dish, 8 × 8 × 2 inches. Beat eggs, milk, baking mix, salt, cayenne pepper and pepper. Spread zucchini in dish; sprinkle with tomatoes and cheese. Pour egg mixture over cheese mixture. Bake uncovered until golden, 45 to 50 minutes. Let stand 10 minutes before serving.

6 servings/about 16 grams protein per serving.

CHEDDAR CHEESE PIE

9-inch Baked Pie Shell (below)
3 cups shredded sharp natural Cheddar
  cheese (about 12 ounces)
1 teaspoon instant minced onion or 3
  tablespoons finely chopped onion
½ teaspoon salt
½ teaspoon dry mustard
½ teaspoon Worcestershire sauce
3 eggs
6 medium tomatoes, peeled
Salt and pepper
2 tablespoons chopped green pepper

Prepare Baked Pie Shell.

Heat oven to 325°. Heat cheese, onion, salt, mustard and Worcestershire sauce over low heat, stirring constantly, until cheese is melted. Remove from heat. In large bowl, beat eggs until foamy; gradually add cheese mixture and continue beating until smooth. Pour into baked pie shell.

Bake until filling is just set, about 25 minutes. Remove pie from oven. Cut tomatoes into thin slices. Overlap slices around edge of pie to form a wreath; sprinkle with salt and pepper. Sprinkle with green pepper. Bake 15 minutes longer.

6 servings/about 20 grams protein per serving.

9-INCH BAKED PIE SHELL

1 cup all-purpose flour*
½ teaspoon salt
⅓ cup plus 1 tablespoon shortening
2 to 3 tablespoons cold water

Heat oven to 475°. Measure flour and salt into bowl. Cut in shortening thoroughly. Sprinkle in water, 1 tablespoon at a time, mixing until flour is moistened and pastry almost cleans side of bowl. Gather into ball; shape into flattened circle.

Roll pastry on floured cloth-covered board to about 2 inches larger than inverted pie pan. Ease into pan. Fold and roll pastry under, even with edge of pan. Flute edge; prick well. Bake 8 to 10 minutes.

* If using self-rising flour, omit salt. Pastry made with self-rising flour differs in flavor and texture.

BAKED ZUCCHINI AND RICE

3 cups thinly sliced unpared zucchini
  (about 4 medium)
½ cup uncooked regular white rice
⅓ cup chopped onion
¼ cup snipped parsley
1 clove garlic, finely chopped
1½ teaspoons salt
Dash of pepper
¾ cup boiling water
3 eggs, beaten
¾ cup milk
1 cup shredded sharp cheese (about 4
  ounces)

Heat oven to 350°. Mix zucchini, rice, onion, parsley, garlic, salt and pepper in large saucepan; add water. Cover and cook over low heat 15 minutes. Remove from heat.

Mix eggs, milk and cheese; stir into zucchini mixture. Pour into greased 1½-quart casserole. Cover and bake about 25 minutes. Uncover and bake 5 minutes longer.

4 servings/about 17 grams protein per serving.

CHEESE FONDUE

2 cups shredded sharp natural Cheddar
  cheese (about 8 ounces)
2 cups shredded natural Swiss cheese*
  (about 8 ounces)
2 tablespoons flour
½ teaspoon salt
¼ teaspoon pepper
1 clove garlic
1 can (12 ounces) beer
Dash of red pepper sauce
1 loaf (1 pound) French bread,
  cut into 1-inch cubes

Mix cheeses, flour, salt and pepper in large
bowl. Rub cut clove of garlic around bottom
and side of earthenware fondue dish, chafing dish or electric skillet; add beer. Heat
slowly; gradually stir in cheese mixture,
adding only 1 cup at a time and stirring
after each addition until cheese is melted.
Stir in pepper sauce. (Mixture should be
thick and smooth.)

Serve immediately over heat (blazer pan of
chafing dish should be over hot water) or in
electric skillet. To eat fondue, spear cube
of French bread with long-handled fork and
dip into cheese mixture. (If fondue becomes
too thick, stir in additional heated beer.)

8 servings/about 20 grams protein per
serving.

* It is important that the Swiss cheese be aged at
least 6 months.

MEXICAN ENCHILADAS

Enchilada Sauce (below)
1 tablespoon salad oil
12 flour tortillas
2 cups shredded mild Cheddar cheese
  (about 8 ounces)
1 cup finely chopped onion
½ teaspoon salt

Heat oven to 375°. Prepare Enchilada
Sauce. Heat oil in skillet; dip each tortilla
into hot oil, then into Enchilada Sauce. Mix
cheese, onion and salt. Place large spoon-
fuls of cheese mixture on each tortilla; roll
up.

Place in ungreased baking dish, 13½ × 9 × 2
or 11¾ × 7½ × 1¾ inches. Pour remaining
Enchilada Sauce over tortillas; sprinkle with
remaining cheese mixture. Bake until heated
through, 20 to 30 minutes.

4 servings/about 22 grams protein per
serving.

ENCHILADA SAUCE

2 tablespoons butter or margarine
2 tablespoons finely chopped onion
1 tablespoon flour
1 clove garlic, finely chopped
1 teaspoon salt
2 teaspoons chili powder
1 can (16 ounces) tomatoes
¼ teaspoon red pepper sauce

Melt butter in skillet. Add onion; cook and
stir until tender. Stir in flour, garlic, salt
and chili powder. Cook, stirring constantly,
until bubbly. Remove from heat; stir in
tomatoes and pepper sauce. Heat to boiling, stirring constantly. Boil and stir 1
minute.

TORTILLA-SOUR CREAM BAKE

1 tablespoon salad oil
¼ cup chopped onion
1 can (16 ounces) tomatoes
½ teaspoon oregano
1 tablespoon pickle relish
1 teaspoon salt
6 corn or flour tortillas
1½ cups shredded Monterey (Jack) or
 mild Cheddar cheese (about 6 ounces)
½ cup dairy sour cream
¼ cup milk

Heat oil in medium skillet. Add onion; cook and stir until tender. Stir in tomatoes, oregano, relish and salt; heat to boiling. Reduce heat; simmer uncovered 10 minutes.

Heat oven to 350°. Spoon 1 to 2 tablespoons tomato sauce on centers of tortillas. Sprinkle half of the cheese over tomato sauce on tortillas; roll tortillas. Place in shallow 1-quart casserole. Pour remaining tomato sauce over tortillas; sprinkle with remaining cheese. Blend sour cream and milk; spread over tortillas. Bake 30 minutes.

4 servings/about 16 grams protein per serving.

WELSH RAREBIT

¾ cup light cream
½ teaspoon dry mustard
½ teaspoon Worcestershire sauce
¼ teaspoon salt
Dash of pepper
4 cups shredded sharp Cheddar cheese
 (about 16 ounces)
6 slices toast

Cook all ingredients except toast over low heat, stirring occasionally, until cheese is melted. Serve immediately over toast.

6 servings/about 21 grams protein per serving.

CHEDDAR CHEESE CHOWDER

1 package (10 ounces) frozen mixed
 vegetables
1 can (10¾ ounces) condensed cream of
 chicken soup
1 soup can milk
1 cup shredded Cheddar cheese (about 4
 ounces)

Cook vegetables as directed on package; drain. Return to saucepan. Stir in soup and milk. Heat through, stirring occasionally. Sprinkle ⅓ cup cheese on each serving.

3 servings, 1⅓ cups each/about 16 grams protein per serving.

GOOD OLE MACARONI AND CHEESE

6 to 7 ounces uncooked elbow macaroni
(about 2 cups)
2 tablespoons grated onion
1 teaspoon salt
¼ teaspoon pepper
3 cups shredded process sharp American
cheese (about 12 ounces)
White Sauce (below)
1 tablespoon butter or margarine

Heat oven to 375°. Cook macaroni as directed on package; drain.

Place half of the macaroni in ungreased 2-quart casserole. Sprinkle with half of the onion, salt, pepper and cheese. Repeat; pour White Sauce over macaroni mixture. Dot with butter.

Cover; bake 30 minutes. Uncover; bake 15 minutes longer.

6 servings/about 21 grams protein per serving.

WHITE SAUCE

2 tablespoons butter or margarine
2 tablespoons flour
½ teaspoon salt
¼ teaspoon pepper
2 cups milk

Melt butter in saucepan over low heat. Blend in flour and seasonings. Cook over low heat, stirring constantly, until mixture is smooth and bubbly. Remove from heat; stir in milk. Heat to boiling, stirring constantly. Boil and stir 1 minute.

EGGPLANT SPAGHETTI

½ cup salad oil
1 eggplant (about 1 pound), cut into
½-inch cubes
½ cup finely chopped onion
1 clove garlic, finely chopped
2 teaspoons parsley flakes
1 can (28 ounces) Italian-style tomatoes
1 can (12 ounces) tomato paste
½ cup red wine
1 can (4 ounces) button mushrooms,
drained
2 teaspoons oregano leaves
1 teaspoon salt
1 teaspoon sugar
16 ounces uncooked spaghetti
1 cup grated Parmesan cheese

Heat oil in Dutch oven over medium-high heat. Add eggplant, onion, garlic and parsley flakes; cook and stir until onion is tender, about 8 minutes. Stir in tomatoes, tomato paste, wine, mushrooms, oregano leaves, salt and sugar; break up tomatoes. Reduce heat; cover and simmer 15 minutes, stirring occasionally.

Cook spaghetti as directed on package; drain. Serve eggplant sauce over spaghetti; sprinkle with cheese.

5 servings/about 21 grams protein per serving.

SCRAMBLED EGGS IN POPOVERS

2 eggs
1 cup milk
1 cup all-purpose flour*
½ teaspoon salt
9 eggs
1 cup cottage cheese with chives
¼ teaspoon salt
3 tablespoons butter or margarine

Heat oven to 450°. Grease 8 medium muffin cups. Beat 2 eggs slightly with rotary beater; add milk, flour and ½ teaspoon salt. Beat just until smooth. Do not overbeat.

Fill muffin cups ¾ full. Bake 20 minutes. Reduce oven temperature to 350°. Bake until deep golden brown, 15 to 20 minutes longer.

During last 15 minutes of baking, beat 9 eggs thoroughly; stir in cottage cheese and ¼ teaspoon salt. Heat butter in large skillet over medium heat until just hot enough to sizzle drop of water. Pour egg mixture into skillet.

Cook over low heat. As mixture begins to set at bottom and side, gently lift cooked portions with spatula so that thin, uncooked portion can flow to bottom. Avoid constant stirring. Cook until eggs are thickened throughout but still moist.

Break open popovers; spoon scrambled eggs into popovers. Nice served with a tomato sauce.

8 servings/about 16 grams protein per serving.

* Self-rising flour can be used in this recipe.

HOME-STYLE SCRAMBLED EGGS

4 eggs
3 tablespoons finely chopped onion
¾ teaspoon salt
3 tablespoons water
¼ cup butter or margarine
1 cup diced tomatoes
1 cup diced cooked potatoes
1 cup diced unpared zucchini

Beat eggs, onion, salt and water. Melt butter in large skillet over medium heat. Add vegetables; cook and stir 2 minutes. Pour egg mixture into skillet.

Cook over low heat. As mixture begins to set at bottom and side, gently lift cooked portions with spatula so that thin, uncooked portion can flow to bottom. Avoid constant stirring. Cook until eggs are thickened throughout but still moist, 3 to 5 minutes.

2 servings/about 16 grams protein per serving.

Note: Home-style Scrambled Eggs are pictured on the front cover—top row, center.

STORING EGGS

Fresh eggs should be stored in refrigerator immediately, large ends up. Use within a week. To refrigerate egg yolks, place in tight-lidded jar, cover with water and seal. They keep 2 to 3 days. Leftover whites can be stored in refrigerator in tightly covered jar a week to 10 days. Or freeze each white in plastic ice cube container; remove to plastic bag for storage.

FRENCH OMELET

Mix 3 eggs with fork until whites and yolks are just blended. In 8-inch skillet or omelet pan, heat about 1 tablespoon butter or margarine over medium-high heat. As butter melts, tilt skillet in all directions to coat side thoroughly. When butter just begins to brown, skillet is hot enough to use.

Quickly pour eggs all at once into skillet. With one hand, start sliding skillet back and forth rapidly over heat. At the same time, stir quickly with fork to spread eggs continuously over bottom of skillet as they thicken. Let stand over heat a few seconds to lightly brown bottom of omelet; do not overcook. (Omelet will continue to cook after folding.)

Tilt skillet; run fork under edge of omelet, then jerk skillet sharply to loosen eggs from bottom of skillet. With fork, fold portion of omelet nearest you just to center. (Allow for portion of omelet to slide up side of skillet.)

Grasp skillet handle with hand; turn omelet onto heated plate, flipping folded portion of omelet over so far side is on bottom. If necessary, tuck sides of omelet under. Season with salt and pepper. If desired, brush omelet with a little butter to make it shine.

1 serving/about 19 grams protein per serving.

SPANISH OMELET

2 teaspoons butter or margarine
1 tablespoon finely chopped green pepper
1 tablespoon finely chopped onion
1 can (8 ounces) tomato sauce
2 teaspoons sugar
1 teaspoon Worcestershire sauce
Dash of cayenne red pepper
2 French Omelets (left)

Melt butter in small saucepan. Add pepper and onion; cook and stir until tender. Stir in tomato sauce and seasonings; heat to boiling. Reduce heat; simmer until sauce is thickened, about 10 minutes. Keep warm over low heat.

Prepare French Omelets. Just before folding omelet, spoon ¼ of the tomato sauce onto each omelet. Serve remaining sauce over omelets.

2 servings/about 20 grams protein per serving.

HANDLING THE EGG WHITES

The lightness of your omelets and soufflés depends on the loving care you give the egg whites. So start with cold eggs—they separate more easily; you don't want even a speck of yolk in the whites. Make sure that bowl and beater are clean, dry, and free of grease. Then allow the egg whites to reach room temperature—they'll beat up faster. The whites should beat up to triple their volume, and your omelets and soufflés will be beautiful.

OMELET WITH MUSHROOM-SHRIMP SAUCE

Puffy Omelet (below)
1 can (10¾ ounces) condensed cream of mushroom soup
½ cup milk
¼ cup finely chopped celery
1 teaspoon finely chopped onion
1 tablespoon lemon juice
3 drops red pepper sauce
1 can (4½ ounces) shrimp, rinsed and drained

Prepare Puffy Omelet. While omelet bakes, heat soup and milk over medium heat, stirring frequently. Stir in celery, onion, lemon juice and pepper sauce. Fold in shrimp. Keep warm over low heat.

When omelet is baked, pour half of the sauce over omelet in skillet. Fold omelet and remove to heated platter; pour remaining sauce over top. Serve immediately.

3 servings/about 22 grams protein per serving.

PUFFY OMELET

4 eggs, separated
¼ cup water
¼ teaspoon salt
⅛ teaspoon pepper
1 tablespoon butter or margarine

Beat egg whites, water and salt until stiff but not dry. Beat egg yolks and pepper until thick and lemon colored. Fold into egg whites.

Heat oven to 325°. Heat butter in 10-inch skillet with ovenproof handle until just hot enough to sizzle drop of water. Pour egg mixture into skillet; level surface gently.

Reduce heat; cook slowly until puffy and light brown on bottom, about 5 minutes. (Lift omelet at edge to judge color.) Place in oven.

Bake until knife inserted in center comes out clean, 12 to 15 minutes. Tip skillet and loosen omelet by slipping pancake turner or spatula under; fold omelet in half, being careful not to break it. Slip onto heated platter.

OMELET CAHUENGA

Puffy Omelet (left)
1 ripe small avocado
¾ cup dairy sour cream
½ teaspoon salt
⅛ teaspoon dill weed
1 large tomato, peeled, diced and drained

Prepare Puffy Omelet. While omelet bakes, peel and dice avocado. Just before serving, heat sour cream, salt and dill weed. Gently stir in tomato; heat 1 minute. Carefully mix in avocado.

When omelet is baked, pour half of the sauce over omelet in skillet. Fold omelet and remove to heated platter; pour remaining sauce over top.

2 servings/about 18 grams protein per serving.

SPINACH FRITTATA

9 eggs
2 tablespoons milk
½ teaspoon salt
½ cup grated Parmesan cheese
2 cups finely chopped fresh spinach
½ cup snipped parsley
½ cup finely chopped onion
1 clove garlic, finely chopped
2 tablespoons salad oil

Beat eggs slightly. Mix in remaining ingredients except oil. Heat oil in 10-inch skillet. Pour egg mixture into skillet.

Cook over low heat. As mixture begins to set at bottom and side, gently lift cooked portions with spatula so that thin, uncooked portion can flow to bottom. Avoid constant stirring. Cook until eggs are thickened throughout but still moist.

5 servings/about 17 grams protein per serving.

DOUBLE-DECK OMELET
WITH CHEESE SAUCE

3 tablespoons butter or margarine
6 eggs, separated
¼ teaspoon cream of tartar
½ teaspoon salt
¼ teaspoon pepper
¼ cup plus 2 tablespoons light cream or
  milk
Cheese Sauce (right)
Parsley or watercress

Heat oven to 350°. Heat two 9-inch glass pie pans in oven with 1½ tablespoons butter in each pan. While butter melts, beat egg whites and cream of tartar until stiff but not dry. Beat egg yolks, salt and pepper until very thick and lemon colored. Beat in cream. Fold into egg whites.

Remove pans from oven; rotate to coat sides with butter. Immediately pour half of the egg mixture into each pan.

Bake until golden brown, 15 to 20 minutes. Tilt pan; ease one omelet onto serving platter. Pour half of the Cheese Sauce over omelet; top with other omelet and remaining Cheese Sauce. Garnish with parsley.

5 servings/about 18 grams protein per serving.

CHEESE SAUCE

¼ cup butter or margarine
¼ cup all-purpose flour
1 teaspoon salt
¼ teaspoon pepper
2 cups milk
1 cup shredded sharp cheese
  (about 4 ounces)

Melt butter in saucepan over low heat. Blend in flour and seasonings. Cook over low heat, stirring constantly, until mixture is smooth and bubbly. Remove from heat; stir in milk. Heat to boiling, stirring constantly. Boil and stir 1 minute. Remove from heat; stir in cheese until melted.

MAHARAJA'S DELIGHT

¼ cup butter or margarine
¾ cup finely chopped onion
¾ teaspoon curry powder
6 eggs
⅓ cup milk or light cream
¾ teaspoon salt
¼ teaspoon pepper
1½ cups cooked rice
1 package (10 ounces) frozen asparagus
  cuts, cooked and drained
2 tablespoons bacon-flavored vegetable
  protein chips

Melt butter in skillet over low heat. Add onion and curry powder; cook and stir until onion is tender.

Combine eggs, milk, salt and pepper; beat with fork until blended. Stir in rice and asparagus; pour mixture into skillet.

Cook over low heat. As mixture begins to set at bottom and side, gently lift cooked portions with spatula so that thin, uncooked portion can flow to bottom. Avoid constant stirring. Cook until eggs are thickened throughout but still moist. Sprinkle with protein chips.

4 servings/about 16 grams protein per serving.

MUSHROOM SHIRRED EGGS

1 can (10¾ ounces) condensed cream of
  mushroom soup
½ teaspoon grated onion
¼ cup milk
6 eggs
2 tablespoons butter or margarine,
  melted
½ cup dry bread crumbs
⅛ teaspoon salt

Heat oven to 350°. Mix soup, onion and milk; spoon about 3 tablespoons into each of 6 ungreased 6-ounce custard cups. Carefully break 1 egg into each cup.

Mix butter, crumbs and salt; sprinkle over eggs. Place cups on baking sheet. Bake 25 to 30 minutes.

3 servings/about 18 grams protein per serving.

THE GOOD EGG

The good egg is a fresh egg—and the true test is in the cracking. A fresh egg will have a clear golden yolk that is firm, round and high. Whether it is deep yellow or pale yellow is merely the result of the type of chicken feed, and the flavor, nutritive value and cooking performance will be the same. The albumen should be thick and white and stand up around the yolk. Quality grading doesn't affect food value, so use Grade A Fresh Fancy eggs for poaching and frying. Put the less costly Grade B eggs into cooked foods.

EGGS IN POTATO NESTS

1 package (5.5 ounces) hash browns
   with onions
3 tablespoons butter or margarine,
   melted
1 egg, beaten
1 teaspoon salt
8 eggs
8 tablespoons light cream or milk

Heat oven to 400°. Cover potatoes with very hot water; let stand 10 minutes. Drain thoroughly.

Mix potatoes, butter, beaten egg and salt. Press about ⅓ cup potato mixture with back of spoon firmly in bottom and up sides of 8 greased 6-ounce custard cups. Place cups on baking sheet.

Bake 20 minutes. Remove from oven. Carefully break 1 egg into each potato nest; pour 1 tablespoon cream over each egg. Bake until eggs are desired doneness, 15 to 18 minutes longer. If necessary, loosen edges of nests with knife; lift to serving plate with 2 forks.

4 servings/about 17 grams protein per serving.

EGGS FOO YUNG

1 tablespoon salad oil
1 medium green pepper, chopped
1 medium onion, chopped
1 cup cleaned cooked shrimp, chopped
1 cup bean sprouts, well drained
1 can (5 ounces) water chestnuts, sliced
2 to 3 tablespoons soy sauce
5 eggs
1 tablespoon salad oil
Hot Soy Sauce (below)

Heat 1 tablespoon salad oil in skillet. Add green pepper and onion; cook and stir until tender. Stir in shrimp, bean sprouts, water chestnuts and soy sauce; heat through. Remove from heat.

Beat eggs until thick and lemon colored, about 5 minutes. Stir vegetable mixture into eggs. Heat 1 tablespoon salad oil in skillet. Pour mixture from cup into skillet, forming patties about 5 inches in diameter. Cook until brown; turn and brown other side. Serve with Hot Soy Sauce.

4 servings/about 17 grams protein per serving.

HOT SOY SAUCE
Combine 2 tablespoons cornstarch, ¼ cup cold water, 2 cups bouillon and 2 tablespoons soy sauce in saucepan. Cook, stirring constantly, until mixture thickens and boils. Boil and stir 1 minute.

EGG CROQUETTES

6 hard-cooked eggs, finely chopped
1 cup creamed cottage cheese
¼ cup soft bread crumbs (packed)
2 tablespoons finely chopped onion
1 teaspoon salt
¼ teaspoon celery salt
¼ teaspoon pepper
Dash of cayenne red pepper
½ cup coarsely chopped nuts
2 tablespoons snipped parsley
⅔ to 1 cup dry bread crumbs
1 egg, slightly beaten
⅓ cup salad oil or shortening

Mix eggs, cottage cheese, soft bread crumbs, onion, salt, celery salt, pepper, cayenne pepper, nuts and parsley just until mixture holds together.

Divide mixture into 12 equal parts; shape each into a ball. Roll in dry bread crumbs. Dip each ball in egg, then roll in dry crumbs again until completely coated. Cover; refrigerate 1 to 2 hours.

Heat oil in large skillet. Fry croquettes until light brown, turning once. Drain. Nice served with a tomato sauce.

6 servings/about 16 grams protein per serving.

CREAMED EGGS WITH SALMON

3 tablespoons butter or margarine
3 tablespoons flour
¼ teaspoon salt
⅛ teaspoon pepper
2¼ cups milk
1 can (7¾ ounces) salmon, drained
6 hard-cooked eggs, quartered
6 slices buttered toast

Melt butter in saucepan over low heat. Blend in flour and seasonings. Cook over low heat, stirring constantly, until mixture is smooth and bubbly. Remove from heat; stir in milk. Heat to boiling, stirring constantly. Boil and stir 1 minute.

Flake salmon, removing bone and skin. Gently stir eggs and salmon into sauce; heat through. Serve over toast.

6 servings/about 19 grams protein per serving.

VARIATION

Creamed Eggs with Tuna: Substitute 1 can (6½ ounces) tuna, drained, for the salmon. About 20 grams protein per serving.

THE HARD-COOKED EGG

Place eggs in saucepan of cold water— enough to cover by at least 1 inch. Heat to boiling; remove from heat and let stand 22 to 24 minutes. Or warm eggs in bowl of hot tap water. Transfer to saucepan of boiling water, reduce heat to below simmering and cook 20 minutes.

EGGS A LA PRINCESS IN CHEESE MUFFIN RING

1 egg
1 cup milk
¼ cup salad oil
2 cups all-purpose flour*
1 cup shredded cheese (about 4 ounces)
2 tablespoons sugar
3 teaspoons baking powder
½ teaspoon salt
Eggs à la Princess (below)

Heat oven to 400°. Beat egg; stir in milk and oil. Mix in flour, cheese, sugar, baking powder and salt just until flour is moistened. Batter should be lumpy. Pour into greased 6½-cup ring mold.

Bake 25 minutes. Unmold on serving platter; serve Eggs à la Princess in center of ring.

6 servings/about 20 grams protein per serving.

EGGS A LA PRINCESS

2 cans (10¾ ounces each) condensed
  cream of mushroom soup
1 tablespoon chopped pimiento
1 cup cooked whole kernel corn, drained
6 hard-cooked eggs, sliced

Heat soup to boiling, stirring frequently. Stir in pimiento and corn; carefully fold in eggs. Keep warm over low heat until ready to serve.

* If using self-rising flour, omit baking powder and salt.

EGGS FLORENTINE

2 packages (10 ounces each) frozen
  chopped spinach
2 tablespoons finely chopped onion
2 tablespoons lemon juice
½ cup shredded Cheddar cheese
4 hard-cooked eggs, sliced
3 tablespoons butter or margarine
3 tablespoons flour
½ teaspoon salt
½ teaspoon dry mustard
¼ teaspoon pepper
2¼ cups milk
½ cup dry bread crumbs
1 tablespoon butter or margarine,
  melted

Heat oven to 400°. Cook spinach as directed on package; drain. Stir in onion and lemon juice. Spread spinach mixture in ungreased baking dish, 8 x 8 x 2 inches. Sprinkle with shredded cheese; top with egg slices.

Melt 3 tablespoons butter in saucepan over low heat. Blend in flour and seasonings. Cook over low heat, stirring constantly, until mixture is smooth and bubbly. Remove from heat; stir in milk. Heat to boiling, stirring constantly. Boil and stir 1 minute. Pour over eggs.

Toss bread crumbs with melted butter; sprinkle over sauce. Bake uncovered 20 minutes.

5 servings/about 16 grams protein per serving.

DEVILED EGGS
WITH CHEESE-SHRIMP SAUCE

9 hard-cooked eggs
3 tablespoons mayonnaise or salad
  dressing
1 tablespoon chopped sweet pickle
2 teaspoons vinegar
½ teaspoon dry mustard
Dash of Worcestershire sauce
Dash of pepper
1 can (4 ounces) mushroom stems and
  pieces, drained
1 can (4½ ounces) shrimp, rinsed and
  drained
¾ cup milk
1 can (11 ounces) condensed Cheddar
  cheese soup
4 cups cooked rice

Cut peeled eggs lengthwise in half. Remove
yolks; mash with fork. Mix yolks, mayonnaise, pickle, vinegar, mustard, Worcestershire sauce and pepper. Fill egg whites with
egg yolk mixture, heaping it up lightly.

Heat oven to 350°. Heat mushrooms,
shrimp, milk and soup just to boiling, stirring occasionally. Spread rice in ungreased
baking dish, 11¾ × 7½ × 1¾ inches. Arrange eggs in 3 rows on top; pour soup
mixture over eggs and rice. Bake uncovered
15 minutes. If desired, garnish with parsley.

8 servings/about 16 grams protein per
serving.

EGGS AU GRATIN EN CASSEROLE

¼ cup butter or margarine
⅓ cup all-purpose flour
¾ teaspoon salt
¼ teaspoon pepper
2 cups water
1 cup milk
2 chicken bouillon cubes
½ teaspoon Worcestershire sauce
1 cup shredded Cheddar cheese (about 4
  ounces)
12 hard-cooked eggs
⅓ cup dry bread crumbs
2 tablespoons butter or margarine,
  melted
⅓ to ½ cup grated Parmesan cheese

Heat oven to 350°. Melt ¼ cup butter in
saucepan. Blend in flour and seasonings.
Cook over low heat, stirring constantly,
until mixture is smooth and bubbly. Remove from heat; stir in water, milk and
bouillon cubes. Heat to boiling, stirring
constantly. Boil and stir 1 minute. Remove
from heat; stir in Worcestershire sauce and
shredded Cheddar cheese until cheese is
melted.

Cut peeled eggs lengthwise in half. Arrange
eggs in ungreased baking dish, 13½ × 9 × 2
inches. Pour hot cheese sauce over eggs.
Toss bread crumbs with 2 tablespoons
melted butter and the Parmesan cheese;
sprinkle over top.

Bake uncovered until mixture bubbles and
crumbs are brown, 20 to 25 minutes.
Garnish with parsley if desired.

8 servings/about 19 grams protein per
serving.

BAKED BEAN CASSEROLE

1 pound dried pea beans (about 2 cups)
2 quarts water
2 teaspoons salt
¾ to 1 cup brown sugar (packed)
1 teaspoon dry mustard
2 teaspoons vinegar
8 whole cloves
1½ teaspoons salt
½ teaspoon pepper
¼ cup water
2 medium onions, sliced
½ teaspoon celery salt
½ cup strong black coffee
2 tablespoons brandy flavoring

Heat beans and 2 quarts water to boiling in Dutch oven; boil gently 2 minutes. Remove from heat; cover and let stand 1 hour. Add 2 teaspoons salt to beans and water. Heat to boiling; reduce heat. Cover and simmer about 1 hour. Add more water during cooking if necessary. Drain beans, reserving liquid. Mix brown sugar, mustard, vinegar, cloves, 1½ teaspoons salt, the pepper and ¼ cup water; heat to boiling.

Heat oven to 350°. Place half of the beans (about 3 cups) in ungreased 2-quart casserole. Cover with half of the onion slices; pour half of the brown sugar mixture over top. Add remaining beans, onion slices, brown sugar mixture and reserved bean liquid. Sprinkle with celery salt.

Cover; bake 1 hour. Uncover; stir in coffee. Bake until excess moisture is absorbed, about 1½ hours longer. During last ½ hour of baking, stir in brandy flavoring.

6 servings/about 18 grams protein per serving.

CRUNCHY BAKED SOYS

6 cups water
1 pound dried soybeans
1 teaspoon salt
1 cup chopped celery
½ cup chopped onion
½ cup chopped green pepper
¼ cup brown sugar (packed)
1 teaspoon dry mustard
½ teaspoon salt
¼ cup salad oil
3 tablespoons dark molasses

Heat water and soybeans to boiling in Dutch oven; boil gently 2 minutes. Remove from heat; cover and let stand 1 hour.

Add 1 teaspoon salt to beans and water. Cover and simmer about 2 hours. Add more water during cooking if necessary. Stir in celery, onion and green pepper; simmer about 1 hour longer. Drain, reserving 1½ cups liquid (if necessary, add water to measure 1½ cups).

Heat oven to 400°. Pour vegetable mixture into ungreased 2-quart casserole. Mix reserved liquid, brown sugar, dry mustard, ½ teaspoon salt, the oil and molasses; stir into beans. Bake uncovered 1 hour.

8 servings/about 19 grams protein per serving.

MEXICANA BEANS

1 can (about 20 ounces) baked beans in tomato sauce
1 cup shredded process sharp American cheese (about 4 ounces)
½ cup diced green pepper

Heat oven to 350°. Mix all ingredients in ungreased 1-quart casserole. Cover; bake 30 minutes. Uncover; bake 15 minutes longer.

4 servings/about 16 grams protein per serving.

ITALIAN BAKED BEANS

1 pound dried lima beans (about 2 cups)
4 cups water
2 teaspoons salt
2 tablespoons butter or margarine
¾ cup chopped onion
¾ cup chopped green pepper
1 clove garlic, finely chopped
1 can (6 ounces) tomato paste
½ cup chopped pitted ripe olives
¼ cup grated Parmesan cheese
2 to 3 teaspoons chili powder
1 teaspoon salt

Heat beans and water to boiling in large saucepan; boil gently 2 minutes. Remove from heat; cover and let stand 1 hour.

Add 2 teaspoons salt to beans and water. Heat to boiling; reduce heat. Cover and simmer 1¼ to 1½ hours, stirring occasionally. Add more water during cooking if necessary. (Do not boil or beans will burst.) Drain beans, reserving 1 cup liquid.

Heat oven to 375°. Melt butter in large skillet. Add onion, green pepper and garlic; cook and stir until onion is tender. Mix in beans, 1 cup reserved liquid, the tomato paste, olives, cheese, chili powder and 1 teaspoon salt. Pour into ungreased 2-quart casserole. Bake uncovered 30 minutes.

6 servings/about 19 grams protein per serving.

THREE-BEAN CASSOULET

1 package (10 ounces) frozen lima beans
3 cans (about 19 ounces each) baked beans (6 cups)
3 cans (about 15 ounces each) kidney beans, drained (5 cups)
1 medium onion, chopped (about ½ cup)
1 can (8 ounces) tomato sauce
½ cup bacon-flavored vegetable protein chips
½ cup catsup
¼ cup brown sugar (packed)
1 tablespoon salt
½ teaspoon pepper
½ teaspoon dry mustard

Heat oven to 400°. Cook lima beans as directed on package. Drain; turn into ungreased 4½-quart casserole. Empty baked beans and kidney beans into casserole. Stir together remaining ingredients; add to beans and mix gently. Bake uncovered 1 hour.

12 servings/about 20 grams protein per serving.

Note: Three-Bean Cassoulet is pictured on the back cover—bottom row, center.

COUNTRY BAKED LIMAS

1 pound dried lima beans (about 2 cups)
1 medium onion, cut into ¼-inch slices
1 cup tomato juice
¼ cup light molasses
2 tablespoons brown sugar
2 tablespoons chili sauce
2 teaspoons salt
1 teaspoon dry mustard
¼ cup bacon-flavored vegetable protein
    chips

Heat beans and enough water to cover to boiling in large saucepan; boil gently 2 minutes. Remove from heat; cover and let stand 1 hour.

Add enough water to cover; heat to boiling. Reduce heat; simmer until tender, about ½ hour.

Heat oven to 300°. Drain beans, reserving liquid. Layer beans and onion slices in ungreased 3-quart casserole.

Mix tomato juice, molasses, brown sugar, chili sauce, salt and mustard; pour over beans and onions. Add enough bean liquid to cover mixture.

Cover and bake about 3½ hours. Uncover; stir in protein chips. Bake until flavors are blended, about 30 minutes longer.

7 servings/about 16 grams protein per serving.

DILLY BEAN SALAD

½ cup mayonnaise or salad dressing
3 tablespoons shredded Cheddar cheese
1 tablespoon prepared mustard
Few drops Worcestershire sauce
1 can (16 ounces) kidney beans, drained
¼ cup diced celery
2 hard-cooked eggs, sliced
3 dill or sweet pickles, chopped
1 small onion, finely chopped
½ teaspoon salt
⅛ teaspoon pepper
2 hard-cooked eggs, quartered
½ cup shredded Cheddar cheese
Salad greens

Mix mayonnaise, 3 tablespoons cheese, the mustard and Worcestershire sauce; refrigerate.

Mix beans, celery, sliced eggs, pickles, onion, salt and pepper; stir in mayonnaise mixture. Garnish with remaining quartered eggs and ½ cup cheese. Serve on greens.

4 servings/about 17 grams protein per serving.

THE BOUNTIFUL BEAN

Two cups or 1 pound of dried beans give you 6 cups of cooked beans. To cut down on cooking time, soak them first. The fast way—heat beans to boiling and boil 2 minutes; then let them stand for an hour and they're ready to cook. Or if you prefer, skip the boiling process and soak beans overnight in a cool place. Both ways give good results.